OH SH*T, I'M 25!

A QUARTER-LIFE CRISIS

Copyright © 2020 by Annie-Claude Ouellet

All rights reserved. Thank you for buying an authorized edition of this book and for complying with copyright laws by not reproducing, scanning, distributing, or storing in a database or retrieval system any part of this book in any form, without prior written permission of the author. This book may not be circulated in any form of binding or cover other than the one in which it is published.

Please note that this is a work of nonfiction based on the life and the unscientific observations of the author. Names might have been changed to protect privacy.

"Your time is limited, so don't waste it living someone else's life. Don't be trapped by dogma—which is living with the results of other people's thinking. Don't let the noise of others' opinions drown out your inner voice. And most important, have the courage to follow your heart and your intuition. They somehow already know what you truly want to become. Everything else is secondary."

-Steve Jobs,

2005 Stanford Commencement Address

I'm so happy someone bought me!

Whether you picked me up because you're experiencing your own quarter-life crisis, I was recommended to you by a friend, you rescued me from the nasty dumpster behind your apartment building, or you're only reading me because the author's best friend forced you to, I'm just glad my words are being shared.

Really, the author thanks you.

INTRODUCTION

The first thing you should know about me is that I'm not a mentor or a life coach, and I won't waste my time, or yours, pretending that I am. The internet is already full of them.

I'm honestly just your average white-girl-next-door and, most of the time, I'm still struggling to get my sh*t together. But aren't we all?

After graduating from university (and dropping out of my master's), I got my first real job. Exciting, or so you would think. No.

I got a boring, entry level, 9 to 5 job where I wasn't living up to my full potential. In fact, I'm pretty sure if I had suddenly missed a whole week of work, no one would have noticed. My salary wasn't allowing me to live the lifestyle my parents had always given me. I wasn't able to afford my daily $4 Starbucks coffee anymore. My love life was meh. Everyone was suddenly relying on dating apps, stringing along eight potential targets at a time. But I had no interest in playing that game. Mainly because I knew my future husband was not going to be found on an app. He would be at home on a Friday night learning how to cook homemade pasta in preparation for when he met me. Future husband, if you are reading this, carbonara is my favourite.

Meanwhile, I kept comparing myself to others who seemed successful and happy on social media, doubting my choices and the direction of my life even more. I wanted what they had. But how would I get it? I didn't know what success and happiness meant to me, and I wasn't sure how to figure it out.

Cue the beginning of a devastating quarter-life crisis.

At that point, I had two options: turn a blind eye to my doubts and hope everything would sort itself out with time, or spend time asking myself the hard questions. I chose to ask the hard questions, to start defining the life I wanted.

I want to share my journey so that you can feel less alone. I know what it's like to feel alone. Everyone is so obsessed with looking good, especially on social media. You go to dinners or parties and everyone talks about their accomplishments, but no one exposes their struggles publicly.

This book is a set of six auto-biographical essays through which I take stock of my life and share my conclusions and revelations. First, I will tell you about how, when I graduated from university and turned 25, all my expectations of adulthood flew out the window, and I got smacked in the face by a quarter-life crisis. Then I will share my musings on career, friendship, romantic relationships, social media, and, finally, the challenges of building self-confidence and setting goals.

I want to help people like me, people who had a 'too comfortable' childhood, to face the adult world effectively. I want to help you take the reins of your lives so you can do something that is more constructive than binge watching the Kardashians hoping to one day to become a millionaire.

I want you to realize that your twenties are the most important years of your life.

In your 20s, your prefrontal cortex is still developing. This is the last decade where your brain can rapidly acquire new information and skills. As a result, this is the most important period to practice the decision-making and reasoning that will mold your executive functions. The experiences and habits that you acquire in your twenties will follow you for the rest of your life. Your personality also changes and develops the most between 20 and 30 years old. Use these years to build your identity! I want you to ask yourself these real questions —and please, try not to have a panic attack:

What do you really want to achieve in your life? What gives you passion? What makes you happy? What can you do for others? Where do you want to build your life? What kind of people do you want to share your life with? At what age do you want to get married, have a house, or start planning for children. Alternatively, do you want any of those things in the first place?

Life offers you a limited time to accomplish your goals. It's hard to realize when you're in your twenties, but time will likely run out on you. There is no good or bad way to live your life. The only life worth living is the life you want, and an unlived life is not worth remembering.

Your 20s are your chance to achieve and unlock your full potential by first realizing (more like accepting) who you truly are and embracing that person.

I WISH I HAD A TOUGHER LIFE

It's September 8, 2018. The blaring of my alarm jolts me awake. As I open my eyes, I suddenly realize I'm 25 years old. I wish I could say that the 364 days that preceded my 25th birthday allowed me to gain some wisdom, maturity, and sense of responsibility, but I'm not here to lie to you. I'm not here to lie to myself.

After a quarter of a century on earth, I should at least be proud of some accomplishment or have some exciting story to tell. But that's not the case.

Instead, reality hits me hard.

I'm 25. No steady job, no house (not even an apartment), no car, no husband, no kids, no passion, and not even any real life plan.

I didn't even realize just how sad this sentence would be before I wrote it. Don't worry, this book will not be *that* dramatic.

In case you were wondering, turning twenty-five has the same effect physically and psychologically as any other birthday. Which is to say none whatsoever. Unfortunately, this means you must, once again, give the same stale line to your Aunt Susan when she calls you on the landline at your parent's house to ask you, "So, twenty-five! How does it feel to be 25?"

I still don't know what kind of response aunts expect to hear when they ask this question. Am I supposed to have become an entire year older and wiser in one day? Obviously, some things have changed, but I didn't have a revelation this morning when my alarm went off. We all know there's no such thing as "new year, new me".

To the great despair of the people close to me, "new me" is not here yet. The 364 days that led to my birthday simply resulted in the following common observation: the older you get, the more incurable hangovers start to become.

At 25, quietly, your increased Tums consumption requires you to make a pharmacy budget (yes, you have a budget now). You realize that you are no longer capable of doing those tequila shots without endangering all of your weekend plans. Strangely, you also experience an urgent need to get to bed before midnight. Not because your Uber is going to transform into a pumpkin, it's just that you're no longer princess material after nine o'clock.

This new unsociability is so powerful that you slowly switch to spending Friday and Saturday nights at home reading a book with a nice, relaxing chamomile tea. Or mint tea, when you're feeling frisky. You are literally becoming your mother, and now you call it a "big night" when your alcohol consumption hits two glasses of wine instead of one. You are now excited by the idea of doing meal prep on Sundays and yoga classes at 6 am. OK. I'm exaggerating a bit, but you catch my drift.

Another revelation, which is way worse for me than my new inability to party, is the appearance of lines on my forehead. Two little lines have now made themselves at home in between my eyebrows. According to my esthetician, they're only expression lines. A normal phenomenon that shouldn't cause me any panic attacks because, apparently, they're not "real wrinkles."

From one perspective, I find them worrying. I probably furrow my brows too much and these wrinkles-to-be are leading me to wonder if I'm too judgemental of others. Am I so bitchy that I'm beginning to develop facial expression wrinkles? Maybe I need an intervention. On one hand, they might simply be a friendly little reminder of my near-sightedness and astigmatism, appearing to tell me I should be wearing my glasses on a regular basis. On the other hand, they sound an internal alarm. Am I past my peak? Will I never be cuter than I am now?

I only just stopped dealing with acne, and I'm already starting to fall apart? Am I doomed to look like a vintage barbie, now and for the rest of my days? How am I supposed to find a mate looking like that? So, I have now put all my hopes in a hundred different types of exfoliators, serums, and creams. I make a potion every night, hoping I will hear "you" when I ask, "Mirror, mirror on the wall, who's the fairest of them all?"

More seriously, reaching the quarter-century mark leads to introspection about your life. You wonder if you studied the right subject, if the relationship you have with your family, your friends, or even the *"whatever is going on"* with that guy from the new trendy dating app, lines up with what you want. This questioning comes at the moment when you have to make important choices like choosing a career and setting out your life plan and goals. In an open world where opportunity abounds and anything is possible, the weight of making a choice creates profound anxiety. There are countless open doors in front of you, but what if you choose the wrong door? It feels like making a decision will set you on a path that might lock you in forever. Imagine spending forever on the wrong path.

The hardest part of this emotional crisis is that no one—except yourself—can provide you with the right answer, if there really is one. Trust me, I've tried. Even Google can't help! During this time, you look up to your friends who are organized, who have things going on for them and have tons of ambitious plans for the future, and somehow you are expected to be able to quell your jealousy. Of course, you're happy and you root for them. At the same time though, it can be difficult not to feel some resentment. You're ashamed of feeling this way but it's hard to ignore when you're surrounded by people and situations that make you feel like you don't measure up.

On the most personal level, you also have to ask yourself if the person you want to be is in line with the person you are. If that's not the case, you must outline, as clearly as possible, the person you want to be. Only then can you dedicate yourself to the projects that will make you happy. You need to start building your own identity if you haven't yet. You have to act on your dreams.

What I'm saying here is, if your dream is to be a personal trainer and the only exercise you do is to get up from the couch to go to the fridge for a soda between two Netflix episodes, maybe it's time to think about getting yourself a gym membership.

Quite often when you leave the classroom behind, you realize there is a significant gap between who you actually are and your ideal self. Your task then becomes fixing your sights on new goals and new dreams. Only when these are connected to your true desires will you be able to shrink this gap. This gap might have been caused by your choice to take a path only to satisfy your parents, but which wasn't in line with your true desires. Juggling university and a part-time job is also demanding, and the loaded schedule at times requires you to put aside your personal projects and hobbies.

If I refer to my own experience, I was often motivated by social ambition. What I mean is that my ambition was the product of environmental pressures: my peers, my family, societal norms. Not arising from my actual desires, this ambition did not necessarily give me any purpose. Until now, my goals were always defined by school. This led me to hit a wall when I graduated; I needed to start coming up with my own goals.

At this age, you must also surrender to the evidence that certain ideas you had conceived for your future aren't going to happen. A change occurs in the way you think about life; you go from a student's vision to that of an adult. The dreams of the past are suddenly no longer important, and you have to accept more realistic ones. Mourning these dreams is not easy, because they have been your driving force for a long part of your life. This happened to me when I finally realized that, because I've never practiced a sport intensely, my dream of making the Winter Olympics was very unlikely. *Quelle surprise!*

Strangely, the quarter-century awakening is also brutal because the number itself becomes imposing. No, it's not fifty, but it is the first time you realize that the years are piling up. You become aware of your own mortality.

At 18, 20, even 22 years old, you still consider yourself young. Your whole life is ahead of you. You have the feeling that, even if you haven't achieved your dreams yet, it'll happen soon. However, when that five sneaks up behind the two, you suddenly realize that you're getting old. Obviously, you start to compare yourself with Joe Schmo and his sister, Flo. Quite often you come to realize that several people have accomplished a lot more than you and, what's worse, you haven't done anything extraordinary. You have the impression that the good years—the years that should be the best in your life—are gone, and you didn't take enough advantage of them. You should have done that camping trip you always dreamed about, you should have taken that internship that could have allowed you to advance your career, and you should've taken university more seriously.

Now, the trips and adventures you want to take are at odds with the pressure and responsibilities of adulthood. Your parents are stressed that you still don't have a stable job or own a house, which makes you stressed too. What's worse, while all your friends are thriving on their paths, you can't help feeling like you're in freefall behind them.

You're probably wondering what could have caused me such a devastating quarter-century crisis. You're not the only one, but I've thought about it for a long time.

I was born in Canada in 1993, when Kim Campbell, a woman, was prime minister of the country (or, as my dad prefers to say, the year the Montreal Canadians brought home the Stanley Cup). Campbell had a pitifully short term in office, but she remains to this day the first and only woman to have led a country in North America. I was born just in time for the beginning of Jean Chrétien's Liberal government, while the country was, as he would confidently proclaim in his uniquely colourful and popular interpretation of the French language, *"Le plus meilleur pays du monde."* The English translation of his catchphrase tells you all you need to know about Chrétien's particular brand of French. "The bestest country in the world." And, he was right. In 1994, Canada topped the United Nations' rankings as the world's most livable country.

I had already won the lottery, but it doesn't stop there. I was also born a woman in a first world country where I had the opportunity to express myself freely and exercise my rights. I was born equal. I was born white and Catholic in a town where everyone was white and Catholic. I was born where my race and religion had never been a problem. I was born in a relatively well off middle-class family, where I was lucky enough to have everything I wanted within reach. I was born in a setting where every chance was given to me.

In elementary and high school, I never experienced a period of bullying. In fact, I had many friends. I was never required to defend myself or to stand up for something. I performed well academically. School was easy for me. I was on several sports teams and, there too, I excelled at a competitive level.

Up to the end of high school, I led a very sheltered life. My parents never denied any of my whims. Whatever toy I wanted, whatever sweet I laid my eyes on in the grocery store, I was given. All I had to do was bat my eyelashes and put on my cutest smile. I was enrolled in everything: soccer, figure skating, dance, hockey, guitar lessons, swimming...everything.

If my heart was no longer in it, I was never forced to finish an activity or a project no matter how much money had been invested in it. My happiness was always their ultimate goal.

I also took part in what we Quebecois call "*la réforme scolaire*" (school reform). The concept behind Quebec's education reform was rooted in increasing the child's self-worth. This reform abolished performance-based recognition and replaced it with an effort-based model. Essentially, this means that whatever my performance was, no one cared. As long as I tried, I was told I was smart and beautiful.

If this model were applied to the NHL, there would be no playoffs, and all the players would receive participation medals at the end of the regular season regardless of their performance.

I'm no psychic, but I can predict that the ratings would not be the same as today's figures. There would be no fights. Imagine hockey without fights! Just thinking about it pains my Canadian heart.

This all felt natural to me. I wasn't ungrateful for the life I was given, but I didn't fully understand just how lucky I was.

My privileged upbringing was a double-edged blade though; I hadn't developed any strength of character, determination, or initiative. Upon reaching adulthood, I realized I lacked so many qualities that are important for making choices and finding your place in the world.

Growing up, my dad used to tell me that being good at everything was my problem. Only later did I realize what he meant. See, I turned out to be good at every activity I tried, but I mastered none. I grew up thinking people were either talented or not. I never thought you could become good through hard work.

The descent began when I finished high school and suddenly, I had to confront adulthood, which was very different from what I had anticipated.

The quarter-century crisis is an emotional crisis characterized by the feeling of not being good enough, by disappointments about relationships or work, by insecurity about the future, and by the impression that everyone is doing better than you.

If you recall, I just told you I grew up in a sheltered environment, which makes me a predictable and easy victim of the quarter-life crisis.

Kids from sheltered upbringings love to make themselves out to be victims.

To fully understand what led me to turn twenty-five while still being jobless, carless, apartment-less, houseless, childless, and unmarried, let me give you a little context. Let's relive the latest years of my life, shall we?

Like so many other little brains filled with imagination, when I was young I had a precise image of what I wanted to be when I grew up.

After finishing high school at the age of 16, I entered Cegep (*Collège d'enseignement général et professionnel)*. In case you are wondering, in Quebec, Canada where I grew up, high school ends at seventeen. After this you go to Cegep for a two to three year college prep or technical program before entering university. It's often compared to a community college, except for the fact that it's required for university admission. So, nothing out of the norm about this plan so far.

Then, I moved to Quebec City to start my bachelor's at eighteen. In my little girl's mind, Quebec was a totally cool and big city. I would finish my master's and graduate by the age of 22 or 23. I hope you realize that I didn't specify either the field of my BA or my master's. I honestly really never thought about it until it was time to apply to Cegep (much too late). After finishing my master's, I needed to find a job and work for a few years. Preferably in a corporate office so that I could wear nice clothes. And a nice lipstick. And carry a briefcase. So professional!

By 25—which is the age I'm at while writing these lines—I needed to be married with my first child on the way. Obviously, at that age, there was no doubt I was going to have a boyfriend. He would even be my first love, who I met the summer following high school at the beach during a gathering of friends. Can I add that Quebec has no beaches? Unless you count the sliver of rocky shore around a lake, a river, or a frigid ocean a beach. I don't. Anyway, I wanted my first love to be my last. How *cliché*!

I also pictured myself taking care of my children, many of them of course. I would cook fresh healthy food from the garden–there's no chance I was going to let preservatives kill them. I would homeschool them so they could learn faster, organize the best birthday theme parties (where I could also dress up), and take them to every sports event. Yes, I wanted to be the coolest soccer mom of all time. But I would be driving a sleek, sexy SUV. No way I was ever going to drive a minivan!

I would also own a big yellow house covered with windows. My "house must include list" included: big windows everywhere, at least one bay window, a pool, and a long patio where I could have my Kool-Aid in the morning.

I was also going to be an important woman. Back then, that could only mean having a company that was mine. Probably one that made candy-flavored lip balms and lip glosses–is it obvious I was a huge Lip Smacker fan? The Coca Cola lip balm was my favourite flavor, no doubt. That was definitely more professional than a Tamagotchi Pet business in my opinion, since I expected people to get tired of them. The pets were so easy to kill. When I was in school, my mom would bring mine to work where she tried to keep it alive by feeding it as often as she could and alternating turns with her co-workers in the emergency room. Still, some days I would come back from school to learn of my Tamagotchi's death and have to start all over again. This is a prime example of first world problems, am I right?

Let me remind you that all of this had to happen by the age of 25.

I've played this scenario on repeat in my head with my barbies every time I carefully took them out of the toy box to make my future come alive. In this fantasy, I was played by my 2001 NSYNC special edition barbie, wearing a tie-dye cropped top and a VIP badge. My husband was played by an overly ripped plastic lifeguard who was always shirtless. At least that explains my strong attraction to men's abs.

I think it's obvious to conclude that this little "dream life" was imagined by the *naïveté* of the light blonde curly-headed little girl that I was. It's impressive, what you can let yourself dream up when you don't take life's limitations into consideration.

But, inevitably, life happened when my friends finally decided that we were too old to play with barbies. One of my life's biggest tragedies!

My problem was that I forgot to modify the expectations I had for myself over time. I actually never spent time thinking about what I wanted my life to be like in the future. For the longest time, life was just as it was, and it was fun.

I didn't need to dream of something to be happy. I let life happen to me. I didn't take control of it. That's probably why, at 25, I found myself disappointed about where I wound up.

To situate you here, the scenario I described was unfortunately only achieved in my playroom.

So, let's get going with the less sugar-coated story which is, unfortunately, the real one.

When I finished high school, I didn't really know what I wanted to be later on or what field of study I wanted to pursue. Partly because I never really had the impression that high school would one day be over but also because the world's most famous question: what do you want to be when you grow up, never triggers anything inside me. When faced with this question (which came more and more as I got older) I would break out in stress sweat. This forced me to say whatever I thought was impressive at the moment: orthodontist, journalist, pharmaceutical sales rep, doctor, business owner.

Perhaps, asking me, "What problem do you want to solve?" or, "What kind of person do you want to be?" would have helped me on my introspective journey.

Let's be real. When a parent asks a kid what he wants to be when he grows up, it's more just for them to analyze if you're ambitious enough to hang around with their kid. I realized this quickly and became good at answering it by saying whatever I assumed older people defined as being "successful".

Unlike most students, I decided to address the situation by living in denial. Exactly like when you feel sick and you have that feeling in your gut that there's something wrong, but you are too scared to go to the doctor because you will actually have to face it. I wasn't ready to face it, so I just decided to wait until maybe a miraculous answer appeared in the sky.

Thus, like every good student who doesn't really know what to do in their college prep program, I enrolled in social science in my hometown's Cegep.

If you're not familiar with what social sciences are in Cegep, it's a bit like the rumors say. Two whole years of relearning what you already learned in high school, aside from the fact that philosophy classes are now a mandatory thing.

In short, it's a nice two-year nap for your brain.

Shockingly, I didn't feel social science was my calling.

I decided to enroll in something a little bit more practical: biomedical analysis in Chicoutimi. New program, new school. I loved biology and chemistry. It was perfect. For a while, I thought that was it.

However, I still felt like something was missing: social interaction.

If around one third of the world is supposed to be introverted, I discovered I was one of the other two thirds. I get energy from being around people. I was also a little annoyed by the fact that I had to give up having long nails, or painting them at all, for the rest of the years to come.

It should come as no surprise that, once again, I changed programs.

I started a bachelor's in consumer sciences at Laval University. I know what you're thinking, this girl is really indecisive. Yes! And, unfortunately, it doesn't end there.

After my first year, I realized that I didn't particularly like my classes. The program was good overall, but what I was learning held no interest for me. It wasn't challenging and I had trouble imagining how I was going to be able to do anything with it.

So, I decided to study marketing, but came right back to consumer sciences, almost as quickly as I started.

At age 24, I finally graduated at the beginning of 2018, to the great relief of my parents.

In reading about my educational pathway, you might notice that I was never particularly certain about what I wanted. I have always had this problem.

I remember when I was very little and would take trips with my family in our spacious, forest green Toyota Sienna (forest green being a very trendy colour in the mid-90s), we made several stops at gas stations. As a family of five, we took a lot of potty breaks. During these stops, at the convenience store, my dad would ask my sister, my brother, and me to choose a treat.

I was always the last to choose.

Quite often, I waffled for several minutes between an Aero mint chocolate bar and a bag of gummies. My dad would slowly grow impatient to get back on the road. Eventually, he would tell me to choose within one minute or we were leaving without me getting a treat. You'll have seen it coming, but I almost always left empty-handed.

The same situation happened when the time came to choose a restaurant. My parents made us choose restaurants we wanted to go to as a family in turn so that everyone would be happy. When it came around to me, my indecisiveness made it so that my sister got two turns to choose. The saddest part of this story is that her favourite restaurant was McDonald's...

Growing up, this indecisiveness gradually crept into all the spheres of my life.

It's called FOMO (fear of missing out) and, little did I know, it was only starting to ruin my life.

When it came to my educational path, I was extremely lucky to have parents that supported me in my choices, encouraged me to follow my frequent changes of mind, and always made me feel their unconditional love. Even though they wished more than once that I could just figure it out.

My last year of university was a very difficult period for me. Not motivated or stimulated by my program, I wasn't happy. I faced no challenges on an academic level. Even the opposite was true. I had the impression that I was wasting my time. I was bored on an intellectual level. I wasn't fulfilling my potential. With a state of mind like that, it was difficult for me to find the motivation to go to my classes, to do my homework, to study, to be involved, and even to interact with my classmates.

I was scared of graduating.

Fortunately, I did graduate.

Finishing university for some people, like me, can be scary. I couldn't be in denial anymore. I still hadn't found an answer to "What do you want to be when you grow up?" I was a grown-up now and it was high time I figured it out. I should have known by this point, and it was keeping me up at night.

As I heard friends talking about their plans after graduation: internships, junior positions, moving to other cities, starting their own businesses, travelling Europe, I did what every student freaking out about leaving university does. I applied to a master's degree.

Yup! There I was, trying to delay the reality check again. But, honestly, it also just felt good to be able to give an answer to everyone when they asked about my post-graduation plans.

In some way, I felt like completing a master's was my only option. I mean, after studying all my life, how was I supposed to start a career?

I spent the last 20 years of my life learning and remembering concepts then vomiting them back onto a piece of paper. That was my only skill: remembering then writing what I remembered. I was pretty damn good at it.

The thing is, I could have probably done anything, but I developed imposter syndrome just by reading the criteria on job applications. Even entry level internship positions seemed daunting.

I felt like if I had an interview, the HR people would be able to smell that I was a fraud. Or, if I got a job, my manager would soon realize that I couldn't actually do any of the things they hired me for. After all, except for the required BA, I didn't have any of the listed skills or experience.

Instead of having a positive mindset, thinking that I would be able to learn on the job, I had panic attacks. Classic.

I was scared that I would feel forever incompetent or that I would never find a job.

Maybe I missed an important class. The one where every other student learned all the necessary skills for those jobs.

My guess was that by doing a master's I would finally learn something I could use— like in daily life, not only to brag about during Trivia. In two years, I wouldn't feel like a fraud. I would be able to actually do the task that was expected of me.

But I did not finish my master's. I came back to my senses and realized if I was to invest so much time and money doing something, it should be something I really want to do and that I was passionate about. Or I could eventually check one box off my "life plan fantasy" by getting my master's during one of my pregnancies. I mean, I would probably need to find something to do while I waited for my husband to come back home with my jar of dill pickles.

The worst part is that I was not having a good time in university despite everyone who kept telling me that those were supposed to be the best years of my life. Like really? If being poor, feeling lost, having no purpose and living in a crappy apartment where the best years of my life, I'm in for a very sad ride.

See, university where I'm from has nothing to do with the experiences those crazy kids always partying in movies have. There are no fraternities, no sororities (at least not for most people), no such thing as choosing the class you want, and definitely no pass—or—fail. People also actually wear clothes during parties in Canada. It's plain old going to class and rushing out of class to attend real life (aka that horrible part-time job that you think about quitting every day but scholarships are a myth so you have to suck it up!).

I think your twenties in general are like biting into an oatmeal raisin cookie thinking it's chocolate chip. No one tells you you're going to feel that lost about who you are and what to do. No one tells you 95% of your decisions will end up being bad ones.

I think what people really miss about these years, and what truly makes them believe they were the best time, was just having no responsibilities and no mortgage, which I get. Or maybe it's not being yelled at all the time when their children can't find something or want a snack while they're reading a book in the storage room, clearly hiding from them.

One truth is that, too often, I just let life happen to me. I was just barely getting by. Whatever happened was fine. Whatever didn't happen was also fine. But deep down, despite not taking any action, I kept hoping something great would miraculously happen to me. I was never ambitious enough to take action.

My school years are a great example of this. Me patiently waiting for my vocation to be written in the sky. Which, let's be honest, it is like waiting for Santa Claus to actually bring you your Christmas gifts.

I always had the impression that I *needed* to get a bachelor's but I was never actually doing it for me. I was always told I could study whatever I wanted and become whoever I wanted to be—as long as it involved a BA. Which is probably why I never truly enjoyed doing it. People never like doing what they feel forced to do. Being able to choose whether you want to do something allows you to discover on your own if you appreciate it or not. For example, when I was young, being obliged to make my bed was real torture. Now, I feel so much excitement and satisfaction from doing it. It almost scares me how much gratification I feel when things are tidy and organized like that

In Quebec where I grew up, most people firmly believe that holding a bachelor's is the key to success. People have this mania of giving more value to the degree than to learning or the skill itself. I grew up being told that with a degree, every door will always be open to me. Of course, a part of this belief is true.

Holding a bachelor's degree allows you to more easily obtain a job with the government, to enter public service with larger salaries, to be more likely to have a 9-to-5 Monday to Friday schedule, to have various social advantages, and to have the "oh so precious and enviable" retirement plan. Even though all that is, in one sense, very attractive, I think that a thoroughly "stable" life is more popular among older generations.

In 2019, becoming a bureaucratic drone, which kills creativity and initiative, isn't attractive to most university graduates. I think what they want to have is an impact, to learn continually and be able to juggle more easily between work and life whether that involves working at 10 am or 10 pm.

The part of this belief that is less true today is that our parents didn't predict what is currently going on in the working world. While both my parents kept receiving job offers before even graduating, every new graduate will tell you, finding a job without experience is nearly impossible.

Today, experience is often more important than education itself in the private sector.

Seriously, at the end of my bachelor's, I began my job search and I even had a hard time getting a call back about volunteer positions. It was a B-R-U-T-A-L awakening!

Absolutely nothing about my undergrad prepared me to enter the job market. I'm not exaggerating. This made me really annoyed thinking back on all the money and the time I wasted on it. I wish my university had a "satisfaction or refund policy".

All the skills I actually needed, I learned by myself online: basic programming skills with WordPress, SEO, Google Ads, Facebook, Instagram, video editing, design, and the list goes on. So many skills that were never covered within my program and that are currently the most important for obtaining a position in marketing or communication.

In the coming years, I am sure that we will witness a decline in university attendance rates and a rise in enrollment on platforms like Udemy if a major change isn't incorporated into the institutions. It's no surprise that I learned more in my online Udemy courses than through the *millions* of scientific articles that my university professors assigned me. I feel that I shouldn't complain since education in Quebec isn't very expensive, even so, I didn't get my money's worth so I'm going to complain anyway.

University should also provide you with one other very important thing: the opportunity to meet people and get involved in several projects, committees and communities. The best thing university offers is the opportunity to connect with people with backgrounds different from our own. It allows us to try new things, and to discover ourselves, not through schoolwork, but through our involvement. This is what we should expect and get from our universities.

So, if you are still in university, the best advice I can offer you is to get involved and take advantage of every extracurricular opportunity.

Try new things, learn new things, create new projects. Find what you're good at and what you're passionate about, then build your certainty around those things. Once you have built them, you will never have to second-guess where you are going again; you'll have all the answers.

It was after dropping out of my master's while working at my first "real job" that I realized I was having a quarter-life crisis. I know it took me a long time. It was actually at a Sunday morning brunch with my gals. When we were in university, we used to chat about our love life and the adventures that happened during the last night out, but that brunch was different. We were all looking for meaning, we were all looking for purpose, and we were all pretty disappointed by the reality of the reality of life after all the promises that we had been made.

My life wasn't what I expected at all and I wasn't who I wanted to be. I felt like I was falling behind. At least while I was in university I was at the same stage as everyone else. Now, I had a few jobs in my back pocket which left me without purpose; I didn't have any spark to follow. I felt like I was running a race with a broken ankle. Sure, I was the only one to blame for it, and I was also the only one who could do something about it. I knew I had to do something about it. I was either facing my reality now or I was facing it at fifty while raging at customer service employees for no reason, doing Botox, and blaming it all on my children for ruining my dreams. Now seems a better time to reckon with my issues.

Contrary to what your high school guidance counselor leads you to believe, figuring out what you want to do when you grow up and, what's more, deciding what you want to do with your life, does not only involve taking a quiz for half an hour. That's just a way to make $100 off of a vulnerable person.

It's a long process and no one talks about it because we are all obsessed with projecting the image that we have our sh*t together when, let's be honest, no one has their sh*t totally together. Twenty-something Britney Spears proved this to the world when she dealt with the pressures she was facing by shaving her head...

There are hours of research and introspection involved in finding the right path and truly (and sadly) nobody has the answer, except for you.

Certain among us are the lucky ones, a little voice deep within them firmly tells them their desires and their dreams, and that enables them to always act accordingly, to surround themselves with a support system that encourages and motivates them on their path. They have built their personality and their certainty sooner.

Others, like me, never really found out what they wanted and just took advantage of the adventure until adulthood came calling and there was no escape. In other words, those who took part in all the university parties until suddenly drinking in the middle of the afternoon is frowned upon. At that time, a great introspection begins in order to complete the search for one's self. It's a difficult quest.

Sometimes, even when you succeed in finding what you want to do, fear of failure holds you back from acting on your desires. The fear of being incapable, the fear of being judged. I'm sure I'm not the only one who feels like this but, after I left university, I felt my support system begin collapsing around me. Obviously, when you are in university at the beginning of your 20's, everyone is cheering you on as enthusiastically as cheerleaders cheering for their crush in high school. Everyone supports you because it's what you should be doing. They all agree that education is a good thing. But weirdly, when you announce to them that you're quitting your "secure" job to start your own ecommmerce business (ecom), all the cheerleaders flee as if they just learned that the quarterback wasn't going to make it to the NFL, but instead was going to end up working at a Home Depot.

Another thing that makes it hard is that, at the same time, you have to fight against yourself. You have to fight against your restrictive beliefs, the ones about what you can and cannot accomplish. Truth is, this process is so hard because we are facing so much more than just trying to find our spark. A lot of our back-thought process is controlled by trying to please everyone and doing what is expected of us. Some of us struggle with that more than others. Personally, I know I struggled with that a lot.

I feel since every chance was given to me, I have no excuses for not being great. People around me put a lot of hope in me, and there's so much pressure from measuring up to those expectations. But when it comes to taking control of your life you should be in charge, not your great great cousin who has an opinion on everything. The thing is, I came to realize that *you* decide both if you can or can't do something.

The sad thing about having a quarter-life crisis is that it's basically a mid-life crisis without the bank account to go and do soul searching.

So, I thought to myself, "How the h*ll am I supposed to get through this crisis with only as much money in my bank account as a four-year-old collects in their piggy bank?"

I started to think, maybe it isn't about finding what I want to do, but who I am.

It became clear that I needed to do something about that the day that I stumbled onto an article online basically saying that the frontal lobe only matures at the end of your 20's. At first, I thought, wow I finally have a good excuse for all my bad decisions. The bad news about this is that it means that after that, all the sucky personality traits you have just become permanent and stain you like spilled coffee on your favourite white blouse. The good news about this is that it turns out that the frontal lobe is sculpted more by a person's environment and experiences and less by their genes. So, I still had time to do something about it.

Although it has always been difficult for me to point at and pin down one big career goal, it has always been easy to say who I wanted to become personality wise. The qualities I was missing in order to become my dream-self were: open mindedness, ambition, confidence. Ok, I guess we all want that. But, I actually decided to go for it.

I decided to solve my quarter-life crisis by working on myself and growing on a personal level. After all, isn't that the most wonderful gift you can give yourself?

Since I'm going to spend the rest of my days with myself, I might as well be happy and in sync with the person that I am.

The same is true for you. I don't want to try to seem like a mother who thinks she's hip and tell you "YOLO," but you really only have one life to live and you are the only person who can make it pleasant and filled with accomplishments.

More important still, I think that everything that happens in your life is a function of how good a person you are and whether you push yourself to be better every day. Your success in your career and in business, the quality of your relationships with your friends, your family and your partner, your ability to be a good parent, and your happiness. Everything comes through personal growth and self-confidence.

I'm far from the life that everyone dreams of at twenty-five but I believed, and I still do, that there is more that I can accomplish than a nine-to-fiver behind a desk waiting for the weekend. Is it building an ecom empire, creating a travel vlog, having a cooking blog, starting my podcast, creating my own skincare line, opening a hostel in Greece? I don't have the magic answer, not for you or for me, but there is more if you decide you want more.

I like to think that it's our dreams that keep us alive. And it's our actions that make them happen.

No matter how small the dreams or how small the actions are: they lead us slowly into becoming who we want to be and, I truly hope, into finding purpose.

Writing this book from Philz Coffee in Palo Alto, in the heart of the mythical Silicon Valley, while sipping on my iced "mint mojitos," I'm aware that my situation isn't bad. I can already hear: Who's that basic white girl crying about having an easy life? And truly, I get where you're coming from.

You might admire me for quitting my job or my master's (I really wonder why you would do such a thing), moving to another country, doing freelancing, or travelling. Or you might not. I am not the person whose name comes immediately to mind when we're talking about success and accomplishment. I don't work for a fancy firm, I don't own a business, I don't have one million followers on social media, and I haven't won any great prizes or accolades.

That being said, a quarter-life crisis ain't about where you're at, but how you feel about who you are and your situation.

I do feel bad about myself and my situation, but I don't feel bad about having a quarter-life crisis. It's a wake up call to go chase who I want to become. And I truly intend to get the most out of it.

Also, I read once that Socrates said, "The unexamined life is not worth living." I guess now both you and I can stop feeling bad about taking time off to do different things instead of rushing in the expected direction. So, let's embrace our quarter-life crises (and be a little pissed about everyone who already knows where they're going)!

DEAR JEFF BEZOS, WHY ISN'T AMAZON SELLING CAREER AND LIFE PURPOSE WITH ONE DAY DELIVERY YET?

SINCERELY, AN OVERWHELMED 20 SOMETHING

As you already know, I was obsessed with barbies when I was young (or younger, I wouldn't want to offend the boomer who might be reading this). What you don't know is that my friend and I used to take baths together where we would bring our barbies with us and use them as marionettes to invent a life for ourselves. Be reassured, we don't do that anymore, neither the bath thing nor the playing with barbies. We would imagine ourselves moving out of our small town to go to university and live together. Then eventually we would find boyfriends, who would become our husbands, then we would have to buy houses next to each other and, after that, we'd obviously both have daughters that would share the same birthday and they too would end up growing up to be best friends.

The only thing we never spent time imagining was what we would actually be doing for a living. *Quel dommage!*

My guess is we probably thought that money actually did grow on trees. Or, that our moms would at some point announce to us that we were the princesses of some small, non-mainstream European country. Perhaps Malta or Liechtenstein. Or, maybe, that we could just type in MOTHERLOAD every time we wanted something just like in the SIMS. Frankly, I still mourn the fact that this isn't a real life hack. Can someone please make this a real life hack so I can MOTHERLOAD my savings account a bit?

I went on not really worrying about what I was going to do until the moment I had to choose a program in university. Ok, I wish I could say that, but the truth is I was even more a mess than that. I went on not really worrying about what I was going to do until I had a deadline for finding a job. Which was when I dropped out of my master's and everybody started to put the "adult" label on me instead of "student." Just like that, I suddenly needed to pay a never-ending list of bills. Who knew you had to pay for things like tenant insurance? I sure wasn't aware that a dozen pieces of furniture from IKEA and some old appliances from Craigslist were worth insuring.

DO I SUCK OR IS IT MY IMPOSTER SYNDROME TALKING?

One of the first challenges I faced after graduating university was the petrifying imposter syndrome. As new grads, we all experience some sort of *imposterism.* We doubt our skills, talents and achievements; we doubt ourselves. That was the kick starter of my quarter-life crisis.

As I was scrolling down all the job offers on LinkedIn and my university jobs portal, paying attention to the never-ending list of criteria for the jobs, I was always left with the feeling that I wasn't good enough. That I hadn't accomplished enough or I lacked all the experiences they were asking for, or the knowledge. Companies really need to stop making us feel shitty with their requirements sections. I might not be the best candidate, but I'm smart enough to realize it doesn't make sense to ask for twenty plus years of experience in social media. Who are you trying to hire? The founder of Doyoulookgood.com? Good luck with that. I don't want to tell anybody how to do their hiring, but that's pretty niche.

The long lists of experiences and qualities intimidated me so much that I felt like it was useless for me to even apply to any job. I was convinced that, even if I was able to get through the interview process, at one point they would find out that I was indeed incompetent, that I was just another fraud. I felt really stupid and thought everybody around me was so much smarter. I was just average at everything, and there's nothing I could do with my averageness. I spent weeks panicking over the fact that if I ever wanted to get a job, I'd have to go back to university, take more classes and get more degrees. I felt overwhelmed. The number of interviews I canceled just a few hours before I was supposed to show up is pretty embarrassing. I was so overwhelmed by the fact that I wasn't smart enough to deserve the job. After all, I had no idea how to do anything. I was afraid to look stupid because I didn't know everything yet. This is how I experienced *imposterism.*

I started to apply to the most entry level jobs I could find. The only ones I felt secure enough to apply to were often internship positions.

Still, I wouldn't get any calls back. Rejections are nothing personal, and have nothing to do with your self-worth, but it's still rejection, and it hurts just as much as scuffing your knees on the gymnasium floor during dodgeball in elementary school. Of course, this just made my imposter syndrome that much worse.

It seems crazy to me that we let ourselves feel this way when we're just as good and just as competent as our peers. We all have doubts about our abilities sometimes, and no one has any clue what they're doing at first.

Nobody knows it all either. And nobody is ever 100% qualified for a job. We just need to overcome our insecurity by being willing and eager to work hard and learn along the way. That's how everyone grows into fitting their position's shoes.

It's hard to think positively because we don't really see how much effort others are putting forward, how much they struggle, how hard they are trying. All we see is the polished version of others, the version they present to the world. It's easy to convince yourself that everyone else possesses natural-born talent, because that's what society values, so that's the façade we tend to hide behind. Don't give in to that pressure. Don't let false assumptions undermine your effort.

Truth be told, almost nobody has any idea what they're doing when they start. They just show up and Google it like everybody else. (But hopefully if you went to Med school, you know what you're doing when you start.)

Applying for jobs was also super-duper hard for me because I had no clue of what I wanted to do or what I was supposed to do. When you graduate from law school, you become a lawyer. When you graduate from consumer sciences, what the fudge can you do with that? I mean, have you ever heard of that program before I mentioned it? Do you know anyone else who graduated from that kind of program? Probably not. So, what can you do when you graduate from that? The answer is: Kind of like everything and nothing at the same time. It's cool, but it's also a curse. I spent hours looking at random job openings, reading the descriptions and hoping that one would finally give me the aha moment I was waiting for: *Aha! that's what I want to do with my life.* That's a lot to ask from a job description.

The moral of the story is: landing an A+ is way easier than landing a good job, or any job really.

GETTING A JOB DOESN'T SOLVE ANYTHING BUT IT HELPS WITH PAYING RENT

I finally landed my first position after a few months of research and a ton of rejection. I was ghosted by random companies. So. Many. Times. (How rude of Lululemon for not considering my application for the CEO position).

At last, I had my first real, adult job. Yay (Just wait, the downfall is coming)!

As I spent a few months working 9-5 from Monday to Friday, I felt unhappy. I felt like I wasn't accomplishing anything relevant with my life. I wasn't fulfilled. I wasn't passionate about what I was doing, and I didn't have any purpose. It wasn't that something was particularly wrong with what I was doing, it just didn't feel quite right. I couldn't stand the fact that I worked my ass off in university just to settle for, let's be real, a tiny paycheck that didn't allow me to maintain the lifestyle my parents had always provided for me. A paycheck that was way below what I made when I was working part-time as a waitress—a job I didn't even need a degree for! Believe it or not, it's really hard having a Whole Foods lifestyle on a McDonald's budget. I couldn't stand the fact that this was what the rest of my life would look like. The same task, the same people, the same desk, the same route to work every day for the next how many decades? Scary. I can sympathize with the brides and grooms who don't show up on their wedding day. I got cold feet; I couldn't settle for this. I did everything right, why wasn't it all that I was promised?

SAYING BYE-BYE TO A JOB IS SOMETIMES THE BRAVEST THING TO DO

I quit. I quit, and I felt guilty. On one hand, I felt guilty that I wasn't able to survive a 9-5 job even if I was plugged into a coffee IV. Meanwhile, all the other generations before me survived wars and economic depressions. What was wrong with me, was I that spoiled?

On the other hand, I felt guilty that maybe I was doing something incredibly wrong and that I should maybe follow the corporate path everybody was selling me, maybe they knew better. After all, they've been there. It's hard to escape the idea of a safe, carved out, tried path, even when it isn't fulfilling. At least it brings security.

I've learned that it's hard knowing when to quit a job. It comes with big insecurities. it's often easier to stay somewhere that's just ok, than to take a chance at pursuing something that you're not even sure exists. I mean, I still didn't know what I wanted to do. All I knew is that I had strong feelings of doubt and uncertainty regarding the path my life was on. When I quit my first job, I was determined to find more purpose, to create a more fulfilling life for myself. After all, I was lucky and special, so I felt entitled to a much grander life than the one I was living.

Sure, I hear you. First jobs are often *sucky*, they'll never be what you dreamed they would be. You have to do the work to get there first, which might make knowing exactly when to quit even harder. If you feel like the sacrifices you're making are worth where you're going, if you feel like you're heading towards your goal, if you can still find meaning in that goal, that's when you know you're making the right sacrifices. You're in a good place. Keep going, mate! If you feel like you're not growing, or you aren't feeling challenged on a day-to-day basis, that's when you quit. By the way, being at the office by 9 o'clock in the morning isn't considered a challenge—I'm talking about being challenged intellectually, pushed beyond your comfort zone. If you feel like your iced coffee is more important than work, that's always a good sign that you should maybe move on to something else. Or maybe it's just an indicator that you might need to adult-up a little. How can I say this better…having your dad's credit card on your Amazon Prime account is nice, but that's not a sustainable way of living.

Thing is, when we graduated from university, we rushed. We rush toward achieving the goal of getting a corporate job (or any job really) because that's what we think we're supposed to do. We try to check boxes. We do this without even taking time to take a breath from our finals, without taking time to really ask ourselves if it's actually something we want. We don't take time to answer the big questions: What kind of life do I want? How much free time do I want? Who do I want to spend time with? What do I want to spend time being great at? What would I be doing if I had more time? What do I want to do for fun? What do I want to achieve in life? We often rush because we're deeply scared of the future and our massive amounts of student debt. We'd rather choose unhappiness over uncertainty only because it seems to tame the anxiety. But we need to be reminded that it's ok to question the path. It's ok to realize that the path you're on isn't the one you actually want to pursue. It's ok to just slow down; there are so many jobs out there we don't even know about yet. Nobody knows better than you, so you better trust your instincts. There is no right path, there's the path that makes us feel whole, alive, and lights us up—whatever that looks like to you.

I didn't get a job for a long time, a very long time actually. I flew away to the US, and it gave me the head space I needed to stop thinking about all the "should" and "would" and "have to," and to ask myself what kind of experiences I really wanted and how I wanted to live my life. I'm not a cat, I only have one life, and I don't want to waste it.

I had no idea whatsoever of what I wanted to do. I just knew I wanted to find meaning, to become something bigger than myself. There were a lot of things I was interested in (but I definitely had a lack of interest for the BA I graduated with). I liked digging into data and thought destroying the gender gap in data science was compelling. More than that, I thought it was necessary. I pondered the fact that people should be more conscious of the ingredients in their skincare and spend hours reading about it. I consider climate change as something important and thought Leonardo Di Caprio probably couldn't do all the work alone, so I should probably tag along. But I didn't feel a clear or a passion for any of these things. I didn't have the urge to dedicate the rest of my life to pursuing any of them. And all I was though was to pursue something I was passionate about, so here I was, with nowhere to go.

I'd talk about my worries about my lack of passion to the people around me but found poor comfort in their, "It's fine, you'll figure it out," and, "Don't worry too much about it." Poor comfort doesn't actually cover it. These statements made me agonize over the feeling that I was the only one struggling to figure out a thirty-five-year plan. Now, I know that everybody else was just better at pretending than I was.

But I wasn't ready to give up just yet.

I kept asking more and more questions to people I admired about how they decided to do what they were doing, but it all seemed pretty impractical. I kept doing more and more online classes, and none of them covered subjects I felt like I would want to pursue full-time. I fell asleep every night reading one of the dozen self-development books I'd bought. I thought the harder I worked at learning the most about multiple things, or the more I tried different things, the closer I would get to finding this mysterious passion everybody was bragging about, the less I would feel like I an imposter, like I wasn't smart enough. I grew stressed about something that's supposed to be simple: a little thing called down time. If I went out to have dinner with friends, I felt bad for not using the time to work, even though I knew that a well-balanced life would allow me to be happier therefore thrive more.

At the same time, all my friends back home, and everyone in the Silicon Valley bubble seemed to be doing things I couldn't measure up to. Everybody was doing the things my parents had expected me to do: getting promotions or manager positions, starting their bizz, being featured in Forbes. They all made it sound so easy. Sure, I was happy for them, I was in awe of the way they were living their lives, but I also lowkey hated them for making me feel exactly like that kid who got picked last during gym class.

San Francisco has always had a weird effect on me. It's my favourite place on earth. When I say that, people often assume I'm a lunatic. Why? The bloody high rent prices (let's be real, the high price of everything), the homelessness, the needles on Market Street, and human poop on the sidewalk are common things. I'm not kidding. The city has its very own Poop Patrol to clean up the streets. I'm not blind to these issues nor is my nose corked to the smell.

San Francisco is also very true to its reputation: everyone is indeed wearing Patagonia fleece and Allbirds shoes, claims to have a passion for either cycling or rock climbing, says they are vegan, only sips artisanal coffee from Blue Bottle, and works either in tech or in VC (yup, that's the description of the basic tech bro of the Bay area).

All that aside, the city is still very charming. The old Victorian Architecture, the breathtaking view of the Golden Gate Bridge from Battery Spencer, the Salt and Straw ice cream, and the people. It's a hub of brilliant, ambitious, curious, empathic people all in pursuit of a greater self and life. They all believe they can bring value to the world. For these reasons, it's the place in the world where I felt for the first time that I could become a better everything, that the small town girl that I was could become bigger than herself. For that, I'll forever be grateful, and I still get chills when I land at the San Francisco International Airport. It's my magical place on earth. Kids have Disneyland, I have San Francisco. So, what if I need to step on a few poops in order to feel that way. But I'm not willing to step on needles.

But magical by no means implies perfect. That's why, sometimes, the ambition and intellectual curiosity of San Franciscans made me feel like I was condemned to career failure. That again, was the imposter syndrome: the worry of not measuring up.

DEBUNKING BELIEFS

At one point in my never-ending pursuit of passion, an absolute phenom and handsome boy (my ex—he probably would want to be described that way, he's the sweet kind, but not the humble type) recommended that I start reading biographies to be inspired. Maybe, by seeing how others had achieved their success, I could find myself. I was desperate, so I gave it a try.

I started devouring biographies, one after the other. I had already read quite a few when I stumbled onto this passage in "Shoe Dog" the biography of Phil Knight, who founded Nike, which totally explains, better than I ever could myself, the feeling that was messing up my gut like bad tacos from a cheap Mexican food truck. This excerpt changed my perspective on life (I'm aware just how basic this sounds):

> *"I'd have found it difficult to say what or who exactly I was or might become. Like all my friends, I wanted to be successful. Unlike my friends I didn't know what it meant. Money? Maybe. Family? House? Sure, if I was lucky. These were the goals I was taught to aspire to, and part of me did*

> *aspire to them, instinctively. But deep down I was searching for something else, something more. I had an aching sense that our time is short, shorter than we know, short as a morning run, and I wanted mine to be meaningful, and purposeful. And creative. And important. Above all… different."*

I had to define what success meant for me. After all, you can't succeed if you don't know what you're chasing. And chasing somebody else's definition of success will always make you feel like an imposter.

Until then, I was trying to pursue a title, the feeling that title would give me. I thought success was an impressive title, a nice bio to add to my Instagram or my LinkedIn. CEO, or founder, or artist. Something that would impress my friends, and my parents, and my future lover, and also totally random strangers on the internet, of course. Oh, and me. I wrongly assumed that success had something to do with money and title. At the end of the day, isn't that what everybody tells you success is? I had attached my self-worth to it, and when you attach your self-worth to your job and salary (or your lack of a job or salary, which was my case when I moved to the US), it can be a pretty destructive recipe for going after the life you want. And honestly, until now, attaching myself to a status wasn't impressing anyone. The truth is nobody cares about what you're doing for work. People only care that we're good and kind, all the rest is extra. If someone cares about what you do for work, you might want to reconsider their relevance in your life, anyway.

Status is just that, a status. If we tie ourselves to it, we're left empty when it goes away. We feel like we're nothing unless we achieve a certain status, and, if and when we get to that point, it becomes extremely difficult to let it go. This makes us fear change, it keeps us from evolving and innovating. You should always seek to build your self-worth on who you are and what you believe in, not your job and how much money you make.

I sat down one afternoon at Blue Bottle Coffee on University Avenue in Palo Alto, and I stayed until I came up with a code I knew I could live by. I stayed until my very fair Canadian skin tone, not used to the California sunshine, couldn't bear it anymore (I'm well acquainted with applying thick and frequent layers of SPF 60). I decided that if I can define what success looks like for me, I could separate the concept from a career or a job. I came up with the idea that, perhaps, success is about loving the life we have. It's about who we want to be as a person. A successful life lies in the kind of life we live day-to-day, in our lifestyle and our daily activities, on who we spend our time with, and the quality of the character of those we surround ourselves with.

It's about the amount of time that we can devote to our friends, family, and hobbies. It doesn't necessarily revolve around work, or if it does, maybe it's more about our abilities to find work that fulfills us, about how our work makes us feel about ourselves.

A successful life, for me, is one in which I can become better everyday, one in which I can experience and learn new things on a daily basis to satisfy my passion for growing. A life that gives me the ability to live and work from anywhere in the world. A life where I have a positive attitude and a big ugly smile towards adversity and challenge (let's just say I have a few teeth that would definitely benefit from braces). A life where I give an attentive ear to the small dreams that slip by my heart, and where I have the courage to double down on them, to honour them. A life where I spend time loving my family and friends. A life where I make people feel good, feel better, feel understood, feel like they belong.

So, if you too have ADD, or if you heard the cute boy next to you at Second Cup say that he was an engineer (I'm also into nerds), and you weren't paying attention in beginning of this chapter, here's what we've learned: Pursuing a career or a job doesn't necessarily give you the "success" you want. We would much rather spend our time building a life we love than a career. If there's one thing I want you to remember from this whole book, it is that success is what you want it to be, whatever makes you happy and fulfilled. You don't have to live up to anybody's expectations or definition of success if they don't bring you a feeling of pure bliss. We've also learned that I'm not the CEO at Lululemon.

Letting go of the idea that the only way I was going to achieve success was through my work title made my whole career path much less stressful.

With that new mindset, a few of the beliefs I had needed to be reviewed. Maybe there were other preconstructed, mainstream ideas that were getting in my way and preventing me from committing to something, I caught myself thinking.

The lie moms tell

That's how I stumbled onto the thought that, maybe, it's not true that we can do anything.

I said what I said. Don't get me wrong here, I think you can do anything and everything you put your mind to (please, highlight that in pink). If there's something you want to do, know that I'm cheering for you. I'm your biggest cheerleader: *Brrr! Is it cold in here?* I think you should even set your goals higher and your dreams bigger. You're courageous, you're resilient, you're smart, you're awesome, and I know you've got this. I believe in the 10 000 hours rule; if you work hard or practice enough at something (10,000 hours), you can become an expert in anything. You can put the A in fantastic. I believe you can be a doctor, a dentist, a lawyer, a software engineer, a data scientist, a journalist, or an ostrich babysitter. You can have your own restaurant, start your own Macrame Etsy shop, start your hard Kombucha empire, even start your AI company doing that AI-ish thing I don't understand. But the thing is, you might not want to do all of this, or any of this for that matter. You might not want to dedicate 10,000 hours getting good at these things. And that's more than ok.

Our time on this beautiful planet is somewhat limited, we can only do a handful of things. If you take time to narrow down your skills to what you love doing, what you're interested in, what you can get paid for, what the world needs, the options get narrow. Maybe we have far fewer options than we've been led to believe, and maybe that's a good thing. Having too many options causes both FOMO and decision-making paralysis. Saying to someone that they can do anything might convince them that they need to do everything and excel at everything, and if they can't, they're not living up to their potential. You can do anything if you want to, but you're not obligated to. I'm taking that weight off your shoulders. It can actually be a stress reliever to close some doors and turn down certain opportunities.

Passion is overrated

I've also come to realize that passion isn't everything. Finding a passion in order to start living your life is plain stupid, like trying to cut your own bangs after a breakup. You'll only find those things if you throw yourself in. I think passion is actually very overrated. Even if you do find it, it might not be a viable solution. Whoever said you need to do what you're passionate about definitely didn't have an expensive taste for French wine, cheese and clothes (oh Sézane dresses!), and a passion for selling lemonade to your neighbours in front of your house. Not all passions can be monetized—at least the lemonade thing wasn't successful in my neighbourhood when I was young.

You're not doing anything wrong if you're not passionate about what you're doing. You can be happy working on things you love or like. I hate the idea that all passion needs to become a hustle. It might actually make your passion turn sour.

Loving, liking or having an interest in something is enough to give it a shot. I actually think passion comes from working hard on something you love or like, then realizing you're good at it from all the work you've put into it. Once you've gone through the period where you think "oh I suck at this," you'll get really good, and that's when you're going to see the impact you and your work have on others. That's when the spark turns into flames. When you have an impact, you see your value, and that's when you might find your passion. As hard as it is to realize, work will always be work. You might be happy with your work, you might like, love or be passionate about what you're doing. But sometimes, work is just work. No matter how much your work is in alignment with who you are. Some tasks will be boring like answering emails, and someday you won't feel like working but rather getting on a plane to St Tropez. It happens to everyone; no passion will magically change that. Sure, finding your passion is a nice thing to achieve, but it shouldn't serve as an excuse to not commit to a path in the meantime. I'm not denying the fact that you can't magically have a passion falling out on your head, just like you magically find $20 in your old winter jacket, but I think life is not so much about finding yourself but creating yourself. Try things you're *just* curious about, it might turn into passion.

Every day is a chance to redesign your life

Deep down, I know what was stressing me out about landing my first job was the importance of the decision I had to make. When you think you can only choose once, and after that you're on the fast track to retirement, there's a lot of pressure on what you decide to do. It feels like there's no turning back.

We feel like the choice we are making now, the job, the career, the field, the company we choose, will define the rest of our life, so we panic at making the choice of our first or second job. But this isn't the way it has to be. Our parents might have done the same thing for 40 years, but nothing is set forever. That's the beauty of life. Things are constantly changing. Just think about fashion; I thank my guardian angel every day for not making padded shoulders a thing again.

We improve ourselves all the time. We learn new things and skills. We meet new people. We stumble on new interests. As a result, our perspective and our values change. What we like to do will change. What fulfills us will change. So, the goals we chase will be moving targets as we evolve. Try as we might, we can't predict what we'll want to do in 10 years. We'll achieve our goals and set new ones. We'll try something, and completely hate it. We'll figure out what we want, and then we'll end up wanting something else. Maybe it will be something similar, or maybe it will be totally different. We'll change career paths because we find new passions, or maybe we'll get bored of our original work and seek bigger challenges. Figuring out what we want is a flawed process. Allow yourself to change your mind and welcome changes with an open heart. No decision is perfect anyway. There might be some better than others, but none are perfect. We need to treat ourselves with more compassion when we fail, when we're wrong, and when we start over. We need to make peace with our uncertainties. Truth is we'll never have it all figured out but we'll always have a chance to do something else. Every day is an opportunity to redesign our lives.

I gave writing a shot a few months ago. I started journaling. I needed journaling because I had a ton of big existential questions I needed to answer. Yup, journaling isn't just a thing for preteen girls who like to ramble about their crushes. The more I wrote, the more I remembered how much I enjoyed writing as a kid. I stopped writing as a kid because all my friends would mock my grammar. I mean, there's practically as many exceptions as there are grammar rules in French. I had a tough time, and I let people get into my head that I was doomed to be bad at it. But I like writing, and there I was writing my thoughts in my journal, realizing maybe I could be good at it. I realized that writing would also allow me to work while travelling, which is exactly the lifestyle I wanted. So, I took online classes on grammar, I started a blog, I wrote articles that I sent to multiple publications in Quebec, I created content for businesses and gave it away for free. And just like that, I built some sort of experience out of thin air and landed my first real gig.

I like writing because I love making people feel things, making them feel understood, like maybe they belong, and there are other people feeling and thinking the way they do. I like writing because it's way easier for me to express myself that way. I don't love writing, I don't have a passion for writing, and I don't think it's my purpose. My attempt at becoming a writer may fail—hopefully, I'll fall less spectacularly than Theranos.

I might become good, but never great. I might find new interests or take new opportunities. I'll roll up my sleeves and do something else. But, worst comes to worst, I'll have to add storytelling to my artillery. At the end, you have to believe that the dots will connect. That all the things you've done and the skills you've developed will turn your spark into something bigger. The dots always connect when you do the things you love.

Your degree doesn't define you

When it came to choosing a job after university, I truly felt lost; none of the dots connected. The only thing I had going for me was a degree in a subject I was barely interested in, and I let it define me. I thought the only thing I could do was something related to my degree, and I would, because of what I had chosen to study, be stuck on the path it shaped for me. Isn't this exactly what stressed us out about deciding which degree we wanted to pursue to start with?

The thing is, your degree isn't nearly as important as you think it is. It's like having a fake ID but the bar you're trying to get into has a back door that's never locked. Sure, if you want to do something related to your field of study, it might make the journey a little easier and quicker. It's also nice to have a path you can go back to if your new plan falls through. But your degree shouldn't make you feel tied to a certain path; that overly expensive piece of paper does not get the last word.

You are not your degree, and you might not even need one to pursue the best path for you. Whatever you're interested in, you can learn the skills you need with online classes or workshops, or by asking to take more tasks related to it at work, or by getting an unpaid position, or reading about it. There's also nothing wrong with re-doing some steps and going back to university. It's hard, and it might be a long route, but it's still better than doing something you're upset about everyday. It's a worthwhile route because it allows you to work on the person you're trying to become and the life you want to have.

IT'S ALL ABOUT CREATING OPPORTUNITIES

> "Waiting for [opportunities] is like waiting for rain in this drought. Useless and disappointing" - Sam (Hilary Duff), A Cinderella Story.

Ok, she didn't say opportunity, I did. We're told from a very young age that if we work hard and are patient, we'll get what we want. This is wrong on so many levels. You have all the power to create opportunities for yourself, and that's amazing because, believe me, no one will hand it over to you. Seriously, your friend might be there to hold your hair after a night out, and your dad might always be there to lend you money after you lost your wallet in the back of a Lyft again, but the only thing they can do is help; only you can make things better for yourself.

Waiting does nothing but make us miserable. When I was in first grade, I was too shy to raise my hand to ask permission to go to the washroom. So I wouldn't. I would sit still until I couldn't sit still and start dancing on my chair to hold my pee. I would shake my tiny little butt from right to left, and left to right, until my teacher gently came to me to bend over and whisper in my ear that I could go to the washroom if I wanted to. Only then, would I go. Somehow, I never peed in my pants in class, which I think is a miracle.

I have unfortunately developed some bladder problems, such as peeing a little when I laugh even though I haven't given birth yet, and I can't seem to hold my pee anymore. It goes from I don't need to go to the washroom to "WHERE ARE THE NEAREST BUSHES" in 30 seconds. Which caused me to lose way too many undies in the wild and pee on my shoes way more often than I would like. I'm definitely not the cute girl my parents think they've raised. Now you're all like, "where is she going with that pee pee story, it's just kind of gross." It's simple: waiting for anything will leave you as miserable as I was in first grade. You can't depend on anyone else. Everyone is busy doing their thing, and nobody can guess what you want for yourself. You need to go out there, and create opportunities. If there's something you think you might be interested in, ask people who are in that field if there's something you can do to help them with. Find a mentor you can go have a coffee with to ask questions, to help you get started in that direction.

The more you put yourself out there, the more "no's" you get, the luckier you get with opportunities. Life gets interesting when you move—things change, you act. For things to change you have to act, and for you to act you have to start.

Don't wait for your teacher, or anyone else, to tell you when you can start your life. Just start, take control of your own life and go. Otherwise, you may also develop bladder problems.

Curiosity is key

I always felt like most people had that one thing that just made their eyes light up. I thought they were all so lucky to know exactly what their unique "thing" was. I never had that. I thought maybe it was a curse, perhaps my great-great-great grandma did something wrong to one of the Salem witches and she decided to curse our whole family. Turns out, maybe it's more like a blessing and, if any witches were involved, they did me a favour. It's an opportunity to take time to ask yourself what you truly want to do. Not having a predetermined answer to this question gives you the opportunity to follow your curiosity, to try all sorts of things, instead of being stuck with tunnel vision. Some people have been saying they were going to be a doctor since they were 5 years old, so much so that they've never stopped and ask themselves if they actually want it.

Maybe there is another option that would fulfill them more. Living a life following your curiosity gives you a chance to build a sense of what you're good at and what you love doing, and create your own uniqueness little by little. To follow the interest you lost where you were in university and the only thing you were doing where the one imposed on you. Above all, it means that you can discover who you want to be and that you can do whatever you want with your life. Nothing is more empowering than that (sexy lace lingerie aside).

WHERE DO I GO FROM HERE?

So, after all that rambling, how do we figure out what we should do if we don't know what direction we want for our lives? I don't know. Sorry.

I don't know because I don't think there's such a thing as a one long-lasting, never changing answer.

I think it starts with listening to the maybes: maybe I could do this or that, maybe that's fun, maybe I can be good at this, maybe I have value to give. It starts with imagining what you could be doing, who you could become. It starts with believing you can make it happen for yourself.

Do the hard things. Do the things that force you to put yourself out there, the things that will help you grow. If they don't pan out, you'll have learned something.

Take more chances. If you're not getting a lot of no's, you're doing something wrong.

Take the higher risk opportunity, or goal you've been thinking about to work on. It doesn't have to be the biggest thing you've ever dreamed of. But do now what you can't do later. Seize the opportunity you won't be able to seize again. Because, as odd and annoying as it may sound, when you have a family, kids, a mortgage, and other adulting things adults have, taking risks becomes, well, riskier. You have people who depend on you, and to care for. You have much more to lose, much more to worry about. So, the time is now.

Things like starting your own business or working for a startup become difficult. Even switching jobs might be more difficult. You have to do those things now, because you will most likely regret not giving everything you had to that one thing that was tickling your heart. We have to take risks. We have to take bigger risks than choosing our food at an Indian restaurant without looking at the spice level. I think we owe it to ourselves, and to the world, to live up to our own aspirations. Try things! Life is for experimenting, for welcoming changes and being open minded about where your journey is taking you. But make a plan to commit to something, anything. One thing that you're interested in or want to get good at. One thing you love or like. Commit to it for let's say 6 months. Give it all you can, you'll become good. If after being good you don't find happiness or fulfillment doing it or, if you don't feel useful, give up. Yes, give up. Commit to something else, but don't ever stop chasing the person you want to become and the things you aspire to do. Don't ever stop putting the time, the energy, the effort and the sweat in becoming that person.

Then, maybe, you'll find out your passion, you'll find your purpose.

Maybe you'll end up changing your career and field of work a dozen or more times in your life. Maybe you won't. Maybe you'll fall seven times before you figure out what you want to do for the rest of your life. Maybe you'll never find one thing to stick to. Maybe setting your own path will fail, or maybe it will make you deeply unhappy. Maybe you'll go back to that corporate job. Any of these outcomes is totally fine. Remember that. You DO NOT have to settle for a life that doesn't make you happy. Don't stop until you find the life that makes you feel you, that makes you fully happy—after all, you cannot fail unless you quit, so keep going and, with time, you will find it.

I don't think it's wrong to pursue traditional markers of ambition or success. You might take this path and live your best life. I do think it's wrong to not take the time to slow down and ask yourself if these markers of ambition and success align with your own values, so be self-aware of the things you want to achieve and create in life. Just don't pursue a career or a job just for the money or the prestige, these factors will only help you to not hate your job, they won't make you love it. Challenging work, responsibility, personal growth, and recognition will. Until you've found that, there's no need to develop tunnel vision in terms of your plan; be flexible so you can take advantage of any opportunity that arises.

If you really have no clue, define what success look like to you. Define the lifestyle you want. Where do you want to live? Do you want a lot of free time? Do you want to be able to work from anywhere in the world? Do you want to work for a big or a small company? What kind of industry? Ask yourself these questions and find work that's align with the answers. We don't hear this as often as we should but it's also totally fine to not be a career-oriented person.

And please, in the meantime, be kind to yourself. Live in the present. When you stress about the fact that you should have chosen another BA or that you've wasted the past years of your lives, you're living too much in the past. When you stress about the fact that you don't have a clear direction for where you're heading, you're living too much in the future. Either way, you're not doing yourself any good. You have to enjoy the process. We're not static, the people around us are not static, the world is not static; your life is going to be a process. Be happy in the moment, in the place you're at. We often overestimate the impact of a boost in our life. There's no deadline for answering the big questions you have about where your life is heading.

As long as we're staying productive and achieving our goals, I promise we'll be fine. We'll be fine because we'll be stacking up opportunities, experiences, and failures— we'll get knowledge that we can reinvest as a form of capital into ourselves.

We'll be culminating in jobs, skills, interests, strengths, and professional resources. If we keep investing in ourselves, we'll be creating a bigger identity capital, and that's the only way to get better equipped for the future, to move forward in the direction we choose for ourselves. Expanding our career tool box is the only way we'll get a better sense of who we're, what we love, what we're good at, and what value we can bring to the world.

Stop chasing a passion (passions are like first lovers, they'll likely faith anyway). Stop waiting for these "answers" to do something. Focus on doing the things you enjoy, and take a shot at following your curiosity— the things you want to try. Take a shot at something, if you do the math, you already have a better chance of finding "what you want to do with your life" if you just take a shot and invest in it.

This is not a "needing to pee and finding your keys in your oversized purse kind of situation." There's no rush. There's no deadline on finding the thing you want to do or achieving *success*. Remember that J.K Rowling was thirty-two when the first book of the Harry Potter series was published, Colonel Sanders was sixty-five when he began KFC, and if you don't make *Forbes 30 under 30*, there's always *Forbes 40 under 40*. Don't worry so much about what you need to achieve but rather about the person you want to become and the ways you help others become better people.

WHY IS EVERYONE HANGING OUT WITHOUT ME? AN ODE TO THE FRIENDSHIPS THAT LAST AND THE ONES THAT GO TO TRASH

"If you're not losing friends, then you're not growing up." At one time, I saw this quote everywhere in my news feeds and, to be honest, I judged several people who used it to justify the fact that their circle of friends was shrinking. I told myself that, for a person who loses friends, the problem was probably related to the person themself. They should simply stop making excuses and start working on their personality. This quote also gives the impression that in order to grow, you absolutely have to lose friends. It insulted me a little. You see, still to this day, I've stayed very close to my childhood friends. In fact, my circle of friends is mostly made up of my childhood friends, and yet I really did grow up. Hopefully, more than my boobs have.

Although this judgement has only been shared in conversations with myself, I still apologize for having made it against some people. Especially because now, I understand. I understand so much! But also, because I'm not 100% sure vengeful spirits don't exist. And, since this seems like a good enough reason not to play *Ouija* and risk ending up in an exorcist movie situation, I might as well confess my impure thoughts just in case hell turns out to be a real thing.

It's true, growing up means you'll lose friends. It took me a while to realize it (mainly because it sucks). In fact, throughout my life, I never really stopped to think about my friendships. Never. Probably because I spent my life surrounded by friends twenty-four hours a day, seven days a week. I worked with friends, studied with friends, lived with friends, and down time was always for friends. If I had a problem, it was more the fact that I wasn't able to be alone enough. Which I attempted to solve in 2017 by challenging myself to spend a semester without going to parties in order to be less codependent, and to find things I really enjoyed doing alone.

The problem was, I was in the midst of an existential crisis, watching the stories of everyone I followed on Instagram enjoying a good old Friday night. Then it struck me: everyone is having parties with dozens of friends...except for me. What? Suddenly I don't have friends anymore? At least that's what my cell phone was trying to tell me. Why am I still paying for an unlimited text package if the only text messages I receive are to tell me that my cell phone bill is ready? Did I do something wrong to someone? Am I no longer cool? Is there something wrong with me?

I didn't lose friends because of some dramatic blow out. There was no big fight. We didn't end up hating each other to death and there was no point where we were no longer able to mix without ending up fighting in a Jell-O pool during a "wet t-shirt" themed event.

I know guys are going to be very disappointed by this but, alas, that's not how it happened!

I have lost friendships in the sense that we are just not as close as we used to be. It's as plain and simple as that. We still love each other, we still hold on to each other, we just see each other less. We write once a year to wish each other "happy birthday" and occasionally to get news (OK, there are also exchanges of nostalgic memes). We don't invite each other out anymore. Not because we don't have fun together, but only because, over time, we don't think about it anymore. Maybe I'm just not invited anymore because my dance moves are really embarrassing. This theory is plausible: I always dance as if no one is looking at me, and never on the beat!

I have moved away from some people for different reasons. When I finished university, my friends left to land in different places around the world. Then, in addition to the distance, the boyfriends, and the full-time jobs, the responsibilities kept adding up. The daily FaceTimes became weekly, then monthly and, finally, very occasional. Without the context that united us at the start—university, work, same geographic location, same circle of friends—we sadly had no common interest. There are also those friends that I lost because they have to be constantly given attention for the friendship to work. Trust me, if you don't need a clingy boyfriend, you don't need a clingier friend.

I also believe that we become more authentic and more confident as we age, and that slowly, this is what causes our circle of friends to shrink. I am guilty of having already changed my opinion and my behaviour for fear of not being accepted by others.

In elementary school, I stopped playing barbie because all my friends told me it was for little girls. In high school I signed up for hip-hop classes, despite the fact that I hated it, just to "be like everyone else." During university, I went to a bunch of music concerts that I didn't really like just to "be in the gang". I was not sure who I was, so I just fell in with whoever was around. I went along with whatever they wanted to do in order to have different experiences. Now that I'm more certain of the things, if I do not like certain attitudes, values, behaviors, or if some quality goes against the person I'm aiming to be, I distance myself from people who show them.

Over time, what you look for in friendship changes, which means that with certain people, it just doesn't click anymore. That's it.

It is not that some friendships are, or become, insignificant. I have friends I'm no longer close with who were once my rocks. Those friendships were exactly what I needed at that time—the ones where we had an unwritten pact to hold each other's hair when necessary.

They also created stories that I will probably tell until I die. Stories that I'm going to tell my grandchildren just to let them know that grandma was once very "cool". Stories like the pyjama evenings where we would talk about our co-workers and exchange our worst date stories until the early hours of the morning; the karaoke evenings where we landed on the scene with unshakable confidence (partly because, after performing "Man, I feel like a woman" and "*J'irais où tu iras*" a hundred times, we had the songs pretty much mastered, thanks to our national icons Shania Twain and Céline Dion); evenings where we would paint our faces with makeup to try to get into bars at 17; the times I cried on the shoulders of these friends about losing (and hating) my first love. Those are the stories that made me.

To this day, these are probably the people who know almost all of my secrets. They are the ones who know too much to be allowed to make a speech on my wedding day!

But, over the years, I have changed. My friends also changed. We have been exposed to different environments, contexts, and challenges. We all discovered new passions and new hobbies, and we invested in new projects. In going our own ways, we also built relationships with new people separate from each other. With some people, these elements served to unite us more and allowed us to continue to grow together. When I learned something new, they were always interested in learning it. They were always down to try new things with me and vice versa. On the other hand, with some people these elements made us completely different. So much so that I don't think we would have been friends if we had met today.

All these changes influenced my expectations and my needs in terms of friendship over time.

Five years ago, all I needed was friends who were ready to share their clothes with me. I remember doing our hair and makeup together for hours before going to the bar looking exactly the same. These friends and I would cluster together in strategic places inside the bar where the highest concentration of cute guys was hoping that the prey would take our bait. These friends were on hand to hear me complain at 4 am (with a *poutine* in hand, of course) about the fact that no guy noticed me in the crowd. I willfully denied the fact that it is difficult to get noticed when you are surrounded by eight girls who are your identical clones, and that it can be intimidating to come and talk to a herd of girls who stay together all the time. Women are for sure one of the most interesting species of this world! While I'm half kidding about this, this situation did happen every other weekend. What I'm trying to say is that if I had fun with someone, that was reason enough to spend time with them. It was enough to consider them my friends and invest effort and time into the friendship. This is no longer the case.

Now I'm 25 years old and it's probably not a surprise to you if you've been reading this far, but I'm looking out for myself... a lot! But in different ways than I was before. I know which spheres I want to explore, I know my values, I know what kind of person I want to become, and I respect my boundaries.

People who will even offer new ways to help me because they too are motivated by my projects-because they want to see me thrive. In turn, I will offer the same level of support to the people in my life.

I realize how important it is to have friends who support you. I realize how much I need people with whom I can be honest and vulnerable.

These friends are hard to find. They're pure gold.

There were two events that made me realize that I had very few friends who fall into this category. First, there was the day I witnessed a conversation between two of my friends about the project of one of our mutual friends, which was to create her own YouTube channel. Their words were rather derogatory. I immediately questioned myself about the friendship I had with these people. Could they not admire the fact that she took the time to put effort into a project that none of us had the courage nor the will to even begin? Why not encourage her while offering her ways to improve? I didn't get how people who were supposed to be her friends were not only unsupportive, but also talking badly about it behind her back. I hate people who dish on others, especially when they're trying. For some reason that I don't know, people who say that are also, generally speaking, never trying anything themselves. It sure is easy to dish on something when you are not trying.

It became even more evident to me that those friends weren't what I needed the day I started my blog. A year or so ago, I started a blog about skincare. I've always loved skincare and thought, since I knew so much about it, that I should share my knowledge so others could benefit from it (not because I have great skin, unfortunately). I was really excited about it but I told almost nobody. See, I had the memory of that nasty conversation in the back of my mind and I was scared those "friends" would treat me the same way. So, slowly, I lost my enthusiasm for the blog, and eventually stopped writing it altogether, which would have never happened if I hadn't been so concerned with being judged by my so-called friends.

It's easy to become friends with people just because you enjoy their company. However, I think it's important to realize that some people you meet will hold you back while others will push you forward, intentionally or not, because of their behaviors and attitudes. Unfortunately, I had to accept the fact that those friends fell into the first category.

Hanging out with negative people will never give you a positive life.

After cutting them out of my life, I realized the true meaning behind the famous quote of the entrepreneur Jim Rohn: "You are the average of the five people you spend the most time with." I'll come back to that later on.

That being said, not everything about friendships after university is bad. They can actually be better. I think that the best thing about friendship in your mid-late twenties is that the ones that you maintain become better and more profound.

My friendships ask more from me today, but I also get a hell of a lot more out of them.

Over time your heart is forced to take more. More memories, more experiences, and more suffering. More suffering means that there's more you need to go through, to talk about. In order to do that, you need to be able to be completely yourself around the people who are close to you. And you need to trust them. You must feel that, at the end of the day, even if everything collapses, your friends are still there. They don't judge you, and they love you no matter what. And this goes both ways.

These days I have difficult and uncomfortable conversations that I didn't necessarily have before. The decisions and actions of my friends have a more long-lasting impact on their lives. I can no longer be silent. I have to tell my friend if I think she's going to marry a loser (think of your average frat bro called Chad, Matt, or Ted) and that she deserves better, even though I know it's going to be a tough conversation.

This is way different than when I was in high school and all of my fights were about having a crush on the same guy and being pissed at each other because one of us bought the same piece of clothing. Believe me, at the time those felt like huge fights. Hormones and teenagers are an intense mix!

I also need to find the strength to be truly and authentically happy for my friends. Especially when they get engaged while I'm having trouble going on a second date with someone. Or when they get their dream job, I'm still trying to find what I love and what I'm good at. Yeah, sometimes I have to reach deeper to be truly happy for those who get the things I'm still struggling to achieve. I wish it came easier to me because it makes me feel like a shitty person. On some level I know it doesn't make me a shitty person, it just makes me human, but that doesn't make it any less difficult.

These relationships built on vulnerability and hard conversations bring me closer to my friends than ever. Even if I have fewer friendships today, they are way more rewarding. These friendships are what Aristotle calls, "the friendships of the good." I know, this is the second time I've dropped a philosopher's quote in this book, but I swear it's not because I'm trying to nerd out about philosophy. Rather, it is the result of three mandatory philosophy classes and the strange ability of my brain to remember only useless tidbits of information. For example, I would probably not be able to give you a summary of a conversation I just had with someone, but I can tell you the exact date and time when a guy I dated told me the dark circles under my eyes were "bad." I can also remember what I was wearing and what I ate for breakfast that day. Yes, I'm that kind of crazy. A small piece of advice: always remember facts like this because you never know when you will need them to win an argument.

Aristotle is probably one of the most famous philosophers. In fact, if you don't know who Aristotle is, I don't want to shame you but instead encourage you to read something other than a book written by a 20-something in crisis (aka this book). Anyway, he says friendships can be grouped into three types.

First are the friendships of utility, where you are on friendly terms with someone because of the mutual benefits you each bring to the table. Those are usually the relationships you maintain with your schoolmates, your business partner, or your colleagues. The friendships of pleasure are the people you are friends with because of the enjoyment they bring. It's usually the people with whom you share hobbies and common interests. And finally, the best and most important, the friendships of the good. They're the friendships based upon respect, appreciation for each other's qualities, and a strong will to aid and assist the other person because you recognize their greatness. I swear they do exist!

The first two relationships are easily broken. They are the ones you start losing very quickly after university. They are driven by utility and pleasure, so they tend to fall by the wayside when the benefit is achieved or a change of common interest occurs. The friendships of the good are the long-lasting ones but they are much harder to find and develop.

Even if moving on from certain friendships is necessary and normal, that doesn't make it easier. Losing friends and seeing your circle shrink is scary and, frankly, it sucks. The fact is, in your early twenties, your friendships take such an important place in your life, that when this is no longer the case, it is destabilizing. Aside from learning, spending time with your friends is pretty much all you have to do. Your friends become the center of your world. They are the people you work with, who you study with, and who you live with. They're basically the family you've chosen.

I have spent years collecting best friends in every aspect of my life. There were friends from high school, university, work, and all the activities in which I was involved. It was almost as if I was trying to win a competition of who has the most friends. I would show up at every event, always trying to connect with even more people. I'm not too sure who I was trying to impress.

Despite having so many friends, I felt incredibly lonely.

I discovered a new definition of loneliness. Up to that point, my definition of loneliness was what an elderly person living in a care home whose relatives never visited must experience. I had no idea that a twenty-five-year-old having a beer with her friends on Friday afternoon and enjoying the sun on a terrace could somehow still feel lonely. Yet, that's exactly what was happening. It's funny how you can chat for hours with people and appreciate their presence without necessarily building connections on a deeper level. This made it clear to me that being alone and being lonely were two completely different things. Being alone is a state of solitude, usually when you decide to distance yourself to do things on your own, for your own good. Being lonely is an emotion.

I started going to parties where, honestly, the only thing I was waiting for was for someone to tell me that they too wanted to go home so it would be socially acceptable for me to leave. I was so done. Brunch, dinner, small gatherings, lonely, lonely, lonely. It was just such a strange and new feeling.

I was feeling a serious lack of connection. You know, the one you have when you go on a date that is "just ok." It's not bad enough to make the date memorable or to give you a story to tell but it's also not exciting enough to make you want to go on a second one. It just leaves you indifferent, empty, and hungry for a deep connection.

I wasn't sad. I just wanted to be understood by the people around me. I wanted people that gave me the same feeling you get when you're listening to a song that just gets you. I learned that loneliness doesn't come from a lack of company, it comes from a lack of connection. At that point, I knew I needed to make new friends. But, Jesus, nobody told me making friends in your mid-late twenties was going to be this hard!

I've always had friends. I'm not saying this to brag. If that was the case, this statement would definitely be a lie. But really, I always had friends. I was never cool. Except maybe that one time when I was ten where I got an electric scooter. Can you imagine having an electric scooter twelve years before Lime was even a thing?

I basked in the fifteen minutes of fame that scooter gave me. But, and some people will resent me for saying this, I also never got bullied. For a long time, I actually believed there was no bullying in my high school. That was before my little brother told me that I was delusional and there was indeed bullying. So, I truly hope that I wasn't the Regina George of my school and that's why I never noticed it. If that's the case, please accept my sincere Canadian apology. I feel the need to specify it's a sincere apology since, even though most people think Canadians are really polite for saying "I'm sorry" all the time, what you might not know is that 50% of those are passive-aggressive, 20% are because we can't own our actions or words, 10% are used to seem polite, 10% are a replacement to "thank you", "pardon me", or "excuse me", and 10% are because we are indeed sorry, but not that sorry.

When I was in elementary school, I made friends with people on my sports teams or during summer camp. Then, their friends also became my friends. Just like that we were a gang. Somehow, we stuck together until the end of high school. After that, most of my friends went off to the same university as me in Quebec City.

Since I always had plenty of friends around me, I never had to "try to make friends". Obviously, that doesn't mean that, in my entire life, I've never made new friends. I did. All the time actually. The difference is that because I never had the need to make new friends, I let people come to me instead of going to them. This was perfect for me since, even though I would describe myself as an extrovert, I'm actually pretty shy until I get comfortable around someone. And, lucky me, in social contexts, I get comfortable right after the first "Hi".

Even though I'm way too shy to go talk to strangers, I'm socially talented. I laugh easily, I'm always smiley, I go along with everything and I don't take myself too seriously. I can talk about literally anything and find it fascinating. I'm able to keep a conversation going even if I don't know much about what the other person is talking about. I don't like talking about myself, so it makes me an amazing listener. I ask a ton of questions about the other person, which always lets them feel good about me and our interaction.

People love talking about themselves, so they just genuinely end up having a good time. I'm also able to be vulnerable enough to make the other person feel quickly connected to me. But not enough that it makes them feel like I'm getting too personal too quickly. Too much of a good thing can become a bad thing, kind of like ice cream if you're lactose intolerant! This is important, you need to remember this because people bond over vulnerability. I don't really know why, but they do. We find people who share their vulnerabilities brave. Those people create a safe place for others to share their own vulnerabilities, they make others feel like it's ok to not always be perfect or to be on top of things so it's easy to instantly feel close to them. I don't intentionally try to share my vulnerabilities or some personal stuff, I just have very few taboos and, with time, I have realized that's what makes people connect with me. Always come into a conversation unapologetically you, unapologetically authentic, unapologetically vulnerable. Plus, it goes without saying that one of the reasons I make friends quickly is that I always share my snacks and give my last piece of gum. Sharing is caring, mate. I'm telling you, people love small gestures, especially when it's food. I made my first friend in university because he offered me a protein bar to help me deal with my noisy stomach.

Wow. Looking back on the last paragraph, I don't think I ever gave myself so many compliments. But, yay, making friends was always super easy for me. Notice how I said, "was easy?" Yup, it was. That is, until now.

Honestly, I'm very bad at "picking up" friends. Since I never had to make the first move, I never worked on those skills. I mean I did, but only for guys. But picking up friends is so much harder than picking up guys. Usually, with guys, I just give them a cute smile and look at them long enough for them to realize I'm into them so they come sauntering over to talk to me. *Easy, breezy, beautiful, Covergirl!* Unfortunately, this technique doesn't seem to work outside of dating. Believe me, don't try it at home. You're just going to end up embarrassed after a girl asks you if you need something in a very, very cold tone.

I suck at picking up friends for one, and only one, reason: it stresses me out so much. I get sweaty and all freaked out about the first sentence. What's a good pickup line for a friend? The stress was only increased by the fact that I was so lonely, and I felt like there was a lot at stake. I've read somewhere that adults with rich, fulfilling friendships live longer than others and I don't intend to die young. I didn't know it, but it turns out I have social anxiety.

It turns out that being a friendly, outgoing person and having social anxiety are not mutually exclusive. For the longest time, I thought only people who have problems making friends were affected by it. But growing up taught me, more than once, that I'm often wrong. I think we feel social anxiety to a certain extent. You might have a fear of being judged, negatively evaluated, or rejected in a social situation. It turns out that I have a fear of not having anything to say and I never knew about it since I never had to lead a conversation. I think it's funny that you might be busy stressing about your social performance while I'm stressing about mine, so in reality neither of us has time to judge how the other performs. Next time, maybe we shouldn't worry too much about it. And, at the end of the day, the people that you are meant to connect with, won't mind your performance. Does it really matter what the people you aren't meant to be close friends with think about you?

Looking back on it, I probably always had a small dose of social anxiety, but I spent so much time focused on keeping busy and making it to the next step in my life that I didn't even notice it. When I'm nervous, I talk. In my younger years I talked a lot. To the point that it even made people think that I'm totally confident and in control of the situation. It all changed when I set foot in the US. My social anxiety became very hard to handle. The language barrier made it even harder. When I arrived in the US, my English sucked. It really did. I was always scared to go talk to someone because I might mess up a word or a sentence and look stupid. A fear that was a 100% the result of me being annoyed when a non-native French speaker mess up the masculine and the feminine while attempting to speak French. It's not "*bonne anniversaire*" or "*bonne matin*".

I mean, I'm not heartless, I get verb tense errors, but gender errors are just too painful to handle. I also didn't want people to notice my accent, zee annoying French accent.

I was scared to not be able to follow up on a conversation because people would speak too fast (or gibberish), or that I wouldn't be able to express my thoughts properly in another language. At that time, I was basically translating every word from French to English in my head before opening my mouth. What made it even harder is Americans themselves! People often compare America to Canada, and except for our economies being so closely tied together, we're nothing alike.

To my big surprise, Americans don't get my brand of sarcasm at all. They take everything seriously and personally. Being infamous for my dry French humour, I suddenly found that I couldn't make a single joke in English. I also insulted a lot of people.

Americans have an obsession with school. In fact, they obsess so much about it, that one of the first questions you get asked when you meet someone new is "where did you go to college?" As a Canadian, I'll never get that. We don't have such a thing as the "Ivy League" (which honestly just sounds like another house in Harry Potter). At least not in Quebec. No, not even McGill, in case you were wondering. So, I ended up insulting a lot of people by not knowing where they went to school. Well, if it wasn't in Gossip Girl i.e., Brown, Harvard, Colombia, Princeton or Yale, of course I wouldn't know it. And then, just like that, because they felt I wasn't worthy of their time, they would lose interest in talking to me and go talk to someone else. The longer it went like this, the more I became stressed about talking to people and making friends. I was stuck.

The older you get, the harder it is to make new friends. When you're in university, there's always an opportunity to meet people whether it's through teamwork, student jobs, parties, events or just being alive and walking on campus.

After university, those occasions become rarer, and when they do happen, you often have some excuse not to take them. Another thing I've noticed is that people are way more open to meeting new people when they're younger. You see, we all get caught up in our routines and responsibilities. We feel like we barely have time to do all the things we want and to see the friends we already have, so why put the effort into meeting new people? All of this makes it a little harder to find opportunities to meet people open for a real conversation. I miss those days where I could make friends by trading Pokémon cards in kindergarten.

Since those occasions became rarer for me, I took my boyfriend's advice, "you go to the gym and to coffee shops every day, just try to talk to one person a day while you're there." Every morning I would walk with confidence into Philz Coffee. I would take a glance at the place and look for the day's prey. Every morning I would walk out without a friend. The same way I would walk out of the gym. Courage. I could never gather enough courage to go talk to someone. Props to every guy who comes up and talks to me. I mean it. Who knew it took so much balls? Not me. The more I would stress out about talking to someone, the more I would sweat, and stress sweat doesn't smell like normal sweat, it's way more disgusting. Then I would realize I was smelly, and it would make me even more nervous so I would chicken out. I was trapped in a never-ending stress circle.

After a few weeks like this, it was obvious that this wasn't gonna go anywhere. Like the Piczo website I created when I was thirteen for people to find good layouts, it was a good idea, but it was poorly executed. I needed to start smaller. That's why I enrolled in classes for stuff I was really into or wanted to try out. At least there would be new people and we would certainly have something in common to talk about which would make it less stressful. Amazingly, this really has been paying off. Except for that one time I enrolled at a yoga studio in Palo Alto only to find out that it was mainly middle-aged dads. They were cool, just not really what I was expecting. I tried everything: I went to a Bumble BFF brunch date, I joined some communities on Facebook, I accepted and extended more invitations, both from online apps and offline acquaintances, and I went to the most interesting events I could find.

All of this made me realize that first dates with "friends" are as stressful as going out on romantic dates. Who would have guesses worries like what to wear would be a thing? You don't want to be the one overdress for a friend date. The worst is when you had a good time and never hear back from them again. *Aie, aie, aie!* I mean, I wasn't interviewing for a potential marriage or for carrying your child, but aren't I at least "good enough" for deep talk over cheap wine on a lonely Thursday night? Rude!

Friendship aside, if there's one piece of advice I can give you to feel less lonely, it is to join a community. It gives you a sense of belonging. And, doing daily acts of kindness also doesn't hurt. Making others happy can benefit you even more than it does them.

I did all of this and I even reached out to people I admired hoping to become friends. I prioritized friendship. Yes, you read right. I slipped into people's DMs because I thought they were cool. The great thing about this is that most of them actually replied. Breaking news, people don't get annoyed at you for sliding in their DMs as long as you're not sending a dick pic or asking for an unwanted date. You don't have to be Joe Jonas sliding into Sophie Turner's DMs for it to work. But, I'll admit, that would probably help!

The thing is, not everyone you meet will be your friend, nor should they be. I didn't let go of certain toxic relationships just to end up in the same place with different people. Friends, like partners, should be chosen with intention.

I have three rules when it comes to making friends. The first rule: always try to go to events or activities alone. Since you don't have anyone to hang out with, you're kind of obligated to put yourself out there. The second rule; always go sit and make friends with the person who resembles you the least. As humans, we are attracted to people who resemble us the most, but they are often the people who have the least to bring us. They won't get you into new hobbies, they won't open you to new ideas or perspectives; they're just comfortable to be around because they are exactly like you. You've probably already read it many times on some inspirational Instagram page: nothing great comes out of staying in your comfort zone. The third and last rule: make friends only with people you admire, and hang out with them as much as possible. Oh, and also, avoid people who have a personality trait you hate the most. Of course, everyone has flaws (me first!), but this is not about finding "perfect friends" if such things exist. It's about not allowing people in your life who have personality traits you wouldn't want to see in yourself. Your friend's flaws slowly become your flaws. Yes, we have come full circle. You are the average of the five people you spend the most time with.

When my little brother was in grade two, he became friends with a classmate my mom disapproved of. So, she called his teacher to ask that my brother not be allowed to sit in class or in a catechesis next to him. She also never allowed him to see him outside of school. Back then I thought this was a little intense. How could you dislike a kid that much? But it wasn't about liking the kid or not. She is a wise woman. My mom was scared my brother would slowly take on some of his personality traits and, knowing how that kid turned out, her fears were founded.

Truth is, the people you surround yourself with are the biggest influence on your behavior and your attitudes as well as your results. Who you are around influences what you're thinking, saying, doing, and, at the end of the day, who you are becoming. They determine the types of conversation that dominate your attention. They are who you're consistently exposed to, therefore you eventually start thinking like they think and behaving as they behave. This is probably nothing new to you. This process is just part of socialisation. Thing is, we are fully aware of the impact our family has had on the person we are today, but we often forget the impact other groups within our environment have on us. I too often forget to take a step back to think about it and I'm sure you do as well. Be aware of who you surround yourself with since they're a part of what makes you, you.

You can't become who you want to be on your own and you can't be happy on your own.

Humans need each other. If you don't surround yourself with people who possess the qualities you admire or are doing what you want to be doing, chances are, you'll never do those things on your own. There's no such thing as a "self-made" anything. We truly are all connected and inspired by each other. We learn, we share, and we become by sharing with others.

I think you can't let your social environment depend on proximity or chances if you want to be truly happy. Define which opinions, attitudes, and life-philosophies you want to believe in and find the people who share them to welcome into your life as friends.

Don't get me wrong about this last part. I don't think friendships should only be practical. Don't be like one of my friends and rate your friends on different characteristics and spend time with the people who have the highest score. That's a little bit extra, overly logical and one-sided. Friendships should still have magic, they should still be grounded in love. But....

Friends are the best tools you have to get through life, to live a better life, and ultimately to have a happy life. Which is, if you're anything like me, your end goal. Hanging out with people who you admire will also help you grow faster in the direction you want to grow. It's not using people, it's surrounding yourself with people who aspire to the same thing as you. Finding your tribe is also crucial in getting through your quarter-life crisis. When you surround yourself with people with whom you feel you can open up and be you, you actually open up and talk about yourself. Through these conversations, you'll slowly realize who you really are. It's almost like having a free therapist—awesome right?

With time and by applying these rules, I became closer to people with whom I shared similar values. And now, if I think of a compliment about someone, I tell them. What a good start for a conversation? I start with small talk, but I don't keep it up for too long. Small talk is good to start a conversation or to look friendly to someone but that's pretty much all it'll bring you.

To make good friends, you have to be genuinely interested in people. Asking them about their childhood, their passions, their goals is how you'll get to truly know them. Not by asking about their weekend which you don't care about while just looking for an opportunity to brag about what you did during yours. By asking genuine questions you get to know someone on a deeper level. You create stronger ties quicker but also, you're more likely to know if their values align with yours and if you could be a good fit. When I started asking questions like this to people, they often told me they weren't prepared for this. That they needed to think about it, and in the end, we ended up having great and meaningful conversations. And who knows, by asking genuine questions to your colleague or your barista, you might find out that you have friends right under your nose.

When it comes to making friends, there's one quote from the movie "We bought a zoo" that I like: "Sometimes all you need is twenty seconds of insane courage. Just literally twenty seconds of just embarrassing bravery. And I promise you, something great will come of it."

Every day, I gather twenty seconds of courage to reach out to someone. All I need (and all you need) to make new friends is twenty seconds of courage to go talk to someone new. Courage is a muscle that needs to be trained. One that is strengthened by use, and with time, will become stronger and then finding your bravery will feel easier. No one is built with an immunity to fear or rejection, but by building your courage, you can achieve so much more. Starting with finding great friends—people who feed your brain and your soul (and your belly).

TURNS OUT NEITHER SANTA CLAUS NOR PRINCE CHARMING ARE REAL, BUT I'M STILL A PRINCESS!

Dear 15 year old Annie,

Hey you. It's me! I mean it's you, the older you. We're twenty-five now (I know, so old), we wear makeup and we've quit wearing our little brother's clothes. Moreover, we're just obsessed with summer dresses these days. Shocking, right? I'd say we turned out to be a 7/10. Also pretty shocking, right? We still have big (huge!) calves, just like the ones of a gym teacher, or a road cyclist. It's not that big of a deal though! We just pretend it's because we're more muscular than the guys we date. Our boobs still haven't really shown up but we're at peace with it. Beauty standards helped us with that since big "peaches" are now trendy (that's what we call butts these days, I find it really cute, you?). I guess all those years of figure skating finally paid off, eh? Or maybe we've just become the good kind of fat, like an avocado.

Anyhow, I hate to break it to you, but we're still single. So very far from our dream of being married by twenty-five. Spoiler alert: we didn't end up dating any of our high school crushes. No, not even you-know-who. Turns out our first boyfriend wasn't meant to be our last, but we're very happy about that. Not every love story is meant to last forever, or even to have a nice ending—that doesn't make those stories any less great, or not worth living. We've dated and loved so many great guys (and some not-so-great guys, but it's our fault we were into that...). We've honestly been really lucky! But oh, buttercup, there's just so much crying coming up for you. You're gonna cry so much that it's gonna feel like you're dehydrated somewhere on a beach in Mexico after a night out with tequila (you're gonna get this one in a few years). But remember that it's a gift to live such beautiful moments that they're worth crying over.

I just wanted to remind you to always keep loving. Fiercely, ruthlessly, naively, and boldly. It's ok to feel things deeper than others. It's ok to be the one who loves more. It's ok to let people know you love them. It's ok to love until you can't love and hope until you can't hope anymore. It's ok to keep holding on and it's ok to let go. There's no such thing as wasted love. So, go out there and give as much as you can. Just be the person who cares. That's what makes you such a good human. You've got a big loyal heart, and it'll break. Boys will break it. Friends will break it. Dreams will break it. Abandoned goals will break it. Put it back together. Keep it open. Have courage and be vulnerable, always. Pack up your heart and go pour out all of your love somewhere else. I promise, one day, you'll be so happy to have kept it open.

I know you're wondering what love is, so let me tell you. Love is hard (harder than algebra). Love is so, so hard. Love is overcoming obstacles, facing challenges, agreeing to disagree, forgiving and understanding what you think you'll never forget or understand. The truth is the more you know someone, the more you'll get to know their flaws and the harder love will get. You'll learn that there's no such thing as a perfect partner, but there's such a thing as imperfectly perfect love. Love is hard. But remember, you can do hard things; hard things are so rewarding. Love is kind and love is patient, it's true. Love is walking the journey of life with someone hand-in-hand. Love is getting a push to accomplish bigger things and having a place to fall back to when they don't pan out as expected. Love is finding a lover that inspires you to become a better version of yourself.

Please, please, please, do me a favour: as you grow older, never doubt the fact that you're an absolutely amazing human being. You're intelligent, you're smart, you're beautiful, you're funny, you're caring, you're brave, your opinions are valid and you have good instincts. Your love is worthy. You are worthy of being loved.

Annie, xx
PS: Be nicer to mom and dad.

I've been daydreaming about love since my 4th birthday party—the day I received a big white princess dress with a pair of sparkling, clear plastic high heels (they were more like sandals to be honest, but they surely made me feel like I was 10 feet tall). That same day, I forced my five-year-old neighbour into a wedding ceremony. In some ways, I think we all let ourselves imagine what falling in love will look like and create expectations based on our fantasies. Especially if, like me, you grew up watching too many Nicholas Sparks movies with your dad, crying with an Orangina in hand—*we're both very emotional people, ok?*

But none of the many scenarios I imagined for the movie *My Idyllic Love Life* happen. I didn't end up marrying my first boyfriend and Nick Jonas married Priyanka Chopra instead of me (I'm still heartbroken and lowkey hoping the Nick Jonas train will come and pick me up at some point).

Here is where I stand: I don't feel like casually dating, I don't feel like being in a committed relationship, and I feel even less like getting married any time soon. I don't know if I'm a few dates or a few years away from finding love, and it's stressful, but it's also pretty awesome—mainly because I can still flirt with that new cute barista at Joe and the Juice, or that cute guy from Hinge, or really anyone, without feeling guilty even though I have no interest in mingling.

Life has been as hard as Miss Trunchbull in Matilda. I carry a lot of broken dreams in my back pocket: a horrible first time, a ton of vicious fights, a recently overcome addiction for *bad boys,* and multiple fractures on my heart. But also, zillions of first kisses (well, not *zillions* of first kisses, my love life has always been pretty PG 13), and butterflies, and blissful moments of dancing in the park and singing in cars. The ups and downs of my love life make me believe that the purpose of life might be to give and receive love, but they also make me extremely single.

The cool thing is, although my longest relationship happened when I was in elementary school (I might be a little pathetic), I have accumulated a fair amount of experience with unsuccessful relationships. That must be worth something, eh? Here's some wisdom of mine, from one friend to another:

WISDOMS FROM 25 YEARS OF HEARTBREAK

On Being Single:

Being single isn't a bad thing. There's nothing wrong with you for being single; you're not a bad person because you aren't in a relationship. Your value will never be determined by whether or not someone picks you. You might find love at 17, or 23 or 35 or 50; you might get more than one shot at love, or you might never find it. It's ok, *c'est la vie*. But I think chances are, you'll find love. And I'm not saying this because, in my particular case, I went to see a psychic who reassured me that I would indeed find love (I may not be religious, but I still need some sort of spirituality to hold on to, ok). How many people do you know in your entourage who have spent their whole life single? Who have never found love? I don't know anyone in this situation. I don't understand this urgency to find love immediately.

True, life is short, but it is also long when you think about it. I'll admit that being single sometimes gets lonely, but people in a relationship also feel lonely from time to time. Trying to find someone to "fix" this feeling won't work.

On Being Single After Twenty-Five:

There's still nothing wrong with you for being single. May you repeat after me: "There's nothing wrong with me!"

I always found it funny how things take a drastic turn when you graduate from university. There's definitely an unspoken social consensus that it is expected you stay single during your university time, and that these years are meant to be your crazy years, whatever that means (it legit feels like people want you to be a sexual hippie). But when you graduated, it's like suddenly you are old, and need to be miraculously married—like yesterday. I'm not even part of the Royal Family and I feel pressure to give my parents an heir.

If one more person asks me *"why is a beautiful girl like you single?"* I'll snap. I'm looking at you, uncle Vernon. Do you know a charming prince somewhere who is tall, kind, intellectually curious and wants to date a girl with an ice cream only diet restriction, who loves self-deprecating humour and spend her time dancing to some old Cascada? No? Well, shut up uncle Vernon!

Being single after twenty-five is stressful. All your relatives love to remind you that at your age, they were already married, plus there's a feeling of scarcity that erupts. It's like we're all playing a musical chairs game and everybody sat down when the music stopped at the end of university and some of us got left out because nobody told us when the music stopped. Meaning, it feels like there are fewer options as the days go by.

It should be a golden rule to never compare yourself to whatever your parents were doing at your age, it's definitely not the same context. At my age, my parents had already been together for 8 years, my dad had already bought his first business (he bought it at 21!!) while my mom was building out their first house. She paid half of the house in cash. IN CASH! The only way I could make this happen for myself right now is if I started an OnlyFans account, but I'm not sure that would be any help with the single situation.

It's normal to be stress about being single, but you don't have to. Single is an awesome stage to be in life. Focus on doing the things you like, learn about yourself, discover who you are and what your interests are and, spend time understanding the world. Focus on being someone not somebody to someone. The rest will follow.

On First Love:

The flames of a first love are meant to blow out. Like most things in life, love takes practice. When was the last time you did something for the first time and you were absolutely the best you could be at it? Probably never. Do you think your instructor at SoulCycle was this bomb athlete the first time she sat on that bike? No, she probably wasn't. It takes a lot of practice to bike and talk (scream) at the same time. I don't want to be a dream crusher, but if you are good at love on your first try, you're the exception not the rule. And most of us are rules, so go brag somewhere else.

Thinking you can just enter the right relationship when you're ready is wrong. You have to build the skills to create a good relationship before you find one. My first love came with a lot of ups and downs, of loving too much, of not enough room to grow, of miscommunication (or lack thereof), and I've learned all of these wrongs from leaving the relationship.

On Having Sex for First Time:

Your first time having sex is always awkward. It's definitely not the most bragable thing especially if both of you were inexperienced. That was certainly the case for me.

I think most people dream about a romantic first time, at least somewhat. Actually, most girls I know did, but the guys just wanted to get to it. Anyway, I was one of these people. No, I didn't expect candles, flowers, or some handwritten poem, that's just weird *dude*. But at the same time, I didn't want it to be in an old Toyota Tercel in a shady spot of the Wal-Mart parking lot.

Unfortunately, my first time in reality wasn't exactly like my fantasies. After what felt like 5 minutes of me wondering to myself, "is this supposed to be so weird?" and "What should I be thinking about?" it finally came to an end. That's when we realized that the condom didn't stay where it was supposed to stay. So we looked. We searched everywhere but couldn't find it. That's when the panic attack hit me: *Is this thing inside the depths of my vagina? Have I become a lost and found box?*

So, there I was, alone in the bathroom of my boyfriend's house trying to search with my fingers for the condom that just got lost in my vagina while trying to contain myself to not wake up his parents sleeping in the room next door. I finally had to agree to let him go fishing, whereas 20 minutes earlier, I refused to be fingered, arguing that I was too shy. Not very romantic.

Now, I know what you're dying to ask. The answer is yes, we did find it, and no visit to the hospital was necessary. And thank God, because all of my neighbours are doctors and that would have made the next neighbourhood BBQ very awkward for my sixteen years old self. Though, it might have made this an even better story to tell you!

The cool thing is, most people don't have a first time that bad, and sex does get better with time. Although, I've discovered it's impossible to undress as easily as the people do in movies, especially with these super skinny jeans! Having a horrible first time with someone doesn't mean you have to trash the relationship or suffer for the rest of your life. Good sex comes from finding out what you like and establishing a relationship where you both have trust and can ask for what you like without judgement.

On Getting Cheated On:

I got cheated on by the first guy I ever loved. When I found out, I put the blame on myself. I kept thinking that if I'd had been funnier, smarter or prettier it would have never happened. He wouldn't have "needed" to go somewhere else. I had met guilt, but it was the first time I met shame.

Shame is this thing in your head that tells you that because you're flawed, you're unworthy of love, of respect, of belonging, of whatever. It was one of the stupidest things I ever felt, being not good enough to be worthy of love, it was complete nonsense and BS, but we can't judge emotions because we can't control them. It certainly took away a big part of my self-esteem.

I decided to stay with him and to forgive him. A lot of people thought I was naïve for staying in that relationship. We stayed together for about six months, until I realized I could forgive but I couldn't forget. Every time he would hold my hand or talk in my ears, it was like she was right there with us. I wasn't angry, frustrated or resentful. I just couldn't forget it. I couldn't be happy in my relationship anymore.

What I've learned from being cheated on is that it says more about the cheater than it says about you. Don't make this about you, it really isn't. I've also learned that it's ok to give everything you can give to make a relationship work, but to accept failure when it doesn't. It isn't a matter of doing what others believe you should do—stay or walk away—but acting in accordance with what you feel is right. I did everything to make it work. It didn't, and, when it was over, I never once looked back. But I didn't regret giving him a second chance either.

On Getting your Sh*t Together:

We all go into a new relationship with insecurities from past relationships. We call that baggage—some of us travel light, and some of us travel heavy. I carried my insecurities from being cheated on with me for a long time.

I started to care deeply about what others thought of me because I didn't like myself. I needed everyone to love me, to do the work for me. So I ended up dating a few guys that weren't good for me. Guys that would tell me that I was right about all my insecurities. Guys that were always pointing out my flaws. Guys that would add more insecurities. And I was genuinely grateful to them. I was grateful to them for being with me even though I was "unlovable." They were treating me badly and I stayed because I didn't think I deserved better. I was miserable and my insecurities just got worse.

What I'm trying to say here, is whatever insecurities you have, work on them before you do anything else. Messes aren't ready to date (yes, even if you're a hot mess). It's toxic of you to project your insecurities on your partner, and it surely isn't love. There just isn't enough makeup out there to cover up all of your insecurities, so they will show in the daylight at some point. Unless you have an insecurity regarding your dark circles then, the Nars concealer is just a bomb.

Insecurities will either ruin your relationship or attract the type of guys who aren't right for you, or good for you. One sure thing is that they're always going to get in the way of your happiness.

Stop making excuses for all your insecurities and do the work. No matter the excuse you're using to explain why you will never be able to change, or how every solution out there is too complicated or expensive, we're not buying it. There's always a solution. Fix what you can't accept and make peace with the aspects you can accept. And if you don't want to fix anything, fine, but stop complaining. Just practice self-love and focus on what you like about yourself. Again, do the darn work. It's not your friends, family, or partner's job to make you love yourself.

You have to truly believe you're amazing and any guy would be lucky to have you, or they'll never believe it. Until then, dating is a complete waste of time, trust me! Whatever you are attracted to or think you need in a partner is actually what you should provide for yourself first. Build an amazing life for yourself and then find someone you want to spend it with.

On Dating Best Friends:

Don't date them at the same time. Just don't.

On Getting Dumped:

Getting dumped sucks. Sometimes, it's just because you feel sad about the idea that someone doesn't want you, and sometimes it's because your heart is absolutely broken, and you miss them. Either way, they both hurt. If someone leaves you, it just wasn't meant to be. Stop blaming yourself for relationships that didn't work. It's not your fault, not everything mixes well together. For example: chips, good; dill pickles, good; chips and dill pickles, nasty crap. Know your value and keep your heart open for the next suitor.

On Dumping Someone:

Dumping someone sucks more than being dumped. I feel like a lot of people are going to disagree with me on this, but you have to know that we Canadians avoid confrontation. It's a hard conversation to have, and most of the time, you don't do it because you don't love the other person, but because you don't see a future with them. Or sometimes, you just have a feeling that there's an even better match somewhere else. You also have to go on living with the idea that maybe you made a mistake when you can't find anyone that compares to your previous partner. The idea that you've made a mistake will come and haunt you from time to time. I think the longer you stay single, the more aggressively it haunts you. Stop living in the past and believe that whatever is meant to happen will happen.

On Letting Go:

Learning to let go of someone or something is one of the best skills to have, especially when we have invested so much into it. It's a skill I wish I'd learned sooner in life. I have wasted so much time holding on to relationships or people only to end up in a *cul-de-sac.* We often hold on because we hope that it'll end up the way we dream too. Whatever you're holding on to doesn't mean it'll end up the way you want to.

When you ask yourself, "do I stick it out?" if you feel like you aren't moving forward, even slowly, or if you feel like you're putting your own happiness aside for someone else's, that's when you let go. When someone doesn't give as much as they take from you, it's time to let go.

Sometimes, a relationship isn't going in the direction we want it to but we stick with the person because we want to make it work. But we're working on it alone. That's when resentment starts to build, and you can't have a functional relationship. That's why you need to let go, even if it's the hardest of all things you've done. Yes, you might end up together at some point in the future—needing to let go doesn't mean the relationship is wrong or bad—but staying in a relationship that is not working at a certain time will cause you a lot of damage. You always need to keep moving forward in your life and your relationship, and you'll see how life pans out.

On Apple Picking

No guys love apple picking. They just don't. Don't be fooled by all these #couplegoals posts online and think your boyfriend is shitty because he doesn't want to go. He's not shitty. What the other girls are doing online to their boyfriends…it's torture. If you love apple picking, leave that poor guy alone and invite your friends instead but don't invite me. I will not stand in an apple orchard in my Uggs for a photoshoot. That being said, I'm always down for a venti PSL no water and coconut milk. Or anything with pumpkin really.

On The One:

There's no such thing as *The One*. That was a hard pill to swallow for me, like fish oil supplement hard to swallow (those capsules are huge). There are around 7.5 billion people in the world; there is definitely more than one person that is a good fit for you. Just like black leggings, if your favourite pair has a tear, there are plenty of other pairs out there that will fit just as well. You just have to make sure they meet Lululemon standards; You deserve the Lululemon of partners!

On Love is all you Need:

Love isn't all you need to make a relationship stick. You also need shared values, aspirations, and goals. Love isn't all you need to be happy; you also need food, air, a habitat, friends, and a bunch of Girl Scout Thin Mints cookies. Mainly Girl Scout Thin Mints actually!

On Timing:

Timing is important. Surprisingly, bad timing isn't only an excuse that the guy you've been seeing and sleeping with for the past 9 months uses when he doesn't want to hurt you but doesn't have the balls to tell you that he doesn't love you. If a guy isn't ready to commit, it really has nothing to do with you (in most cases). I think guys just aren't like girls. While we can juggle two things at the same time—building our life and working on a relationship—not everybody can. Some people need to be stable before they can commit to anything. Love is about finding the right person at the right time who wants the same things as you. And being sexually compatible doesn't hurt either. If you don't want the same things at the same time, it won't work. If a guy tells you it just isn't a good time, listen to him. In the meantime, someone please tell guys they don't need to be a full bread winner or something before they can open up to a relationship, that's so 1920's. It's not your job to make them change their perspectives.

On Jealousy:

Jealousy is part of the human experience. You'll be jealous from time to time and your partner will get jealous from time to time. It's important to recognize that it's an emotion and nothing more than that. You can't control how you feel, and you shouldn't feel bad for having these emotions. But you can control your reactions. Don't overreact and read too much into something. Don't let it weigh on you. Don't believe the story your jealousy tells you. Allowing yourself to be overcome by it is just plain weakness. And we ain't weak (except when there's 25% sales at Anthropologie). It's going to seep into your relationship and cause problems.

While we're at it, don't go and try to dig up some dirt on your partner's social media account or text messages. You're going to find exactly what you're looking for, even if it doesn't exist!

On Change:

People change because they want to, not because you want them to. If you can picture yourself being happy forever with your partner if he never changes, great. If you can't, he's not the right bro for you! Move on.

On Having a Type:

Sometimes, you don't go out on dates because you assume a person just isn't your type. Well, if you're still single, dating your type hasn't gotten you very far, right? You have to be open minded, like me when I gave a second chance to beef tartar—I still cringe every time I remember the taste. But maybe you're wrong about what type of person you actually need. We create a checklist about what we think we need and I get it, we need something to filter all these guys on dating apps, but we end up dating the same people over and over instead of going with feelings. Date different types of guys, give a chance to the runner, date the cool guy, the nerdy one, or the athlete; there's no right or wrong to the learning process and it might actually surprise you. Sometimes, we know what we want but we're blind to what we need.

On Opposites Attract:

There's are opposite and definitely confusing sayings when it comes to love: "birds of a feather stick together" and "opposites attract". They're both true, but "birds of a feather stick together" rings more true to me. While having opposite interests and personalities makes the relationship more interesting, it's way easier to be with someone who shares your values, your morals, your goals and a similar background. It's just easier to find someone who's as excited as you're about Christmas, without having to explain why Christmas is fun (or whatever holiday you might enjoy). It's easier to be with someone who cares about the same things as you do than constantly having to explain to them why they should care. Interests are easier to change then values, morals, and goals. Life is easier when you don't have to translate your soul all the time.

On Growing Together and Apart:

This one I learned from Negar, my Lyft driver on my way to the Wayfare Tavern in San Francisco, and I told her I would put it in the book. Here it is Negar!

According to her, the secret ingredient in the recipe for a great relationship is to grow together and to grow apart. You need to spend quality time with yourself away from your partner or your relationship will stagnate. That's why we hear some random old dude at a creepy bar telling his old mates that there's nothing exciting about marriage. It's important to spend time on self-improvement and grow as an individual. Whether it's taking classes, being part of your community, or a club, or a sport. Then you can bring what you've learned, what excites you, into the relationship so that it makes you both grow. Find someone you can grow with, always.

On Red Flags:

The infamous red flags. In order to protect ourselves, we grow up being told to look for red flags. Our grandmas told our moms, our moms told us, and we took it to heart. If you're looking to be in a committed relationship, the fact that a guy is not on the same page as you is a red flag. That being said, if you find someone who makes your knees goes weak and they have baggage but are ready to work on it, it's ok. Unless that baggage is an ex he's still mourning over, that's not something you want to mess with.

Relationships are work and there's nothing wrong with being willing to meet a person where they are. This can be a huge bonding process and it's an amazing gift you can give to someone you care about. Also, it's really nice that your friend warned you about *how bad this guy you're dating is,* I mean what are friends for if not for this? But I think we're all capable of being both great and horrible partners depending on the type of relationship and what the other person brings out in us. I think we all have a Karen asleep inside of us and some people just bring the *Karen who wants to see the manager* out of you.

Bad personal hygiene, being rude to the waiter, leaving poor tips to the waiter, being racist, ageist, or sexist, saying cheating isn't "that big of a deal," gossiping to their mom about EVERYTHING in the relationship, and talking about their ex as crazy (they're probably the crazy one) are not just red flags, they're deal breakers, get out of there ASAP!

On Standards:

Your standards aren't too high. Don't ever, ever lower your standards, even if you've been desperate for months, spending all your weekends crying while binge watching *Friends* and binge eating pints of Häagen Dazs Rocky Road ice cream (yup, personal experience here). You shouldn't settle for someone you just have lukewarm feelings for either. However, I think it's important to know the difference between having standards and being picky.

Being picky is focusing on a particular aspect of someone even though you have a great connection. These may include the school where he studies, what he's doing for work, or the type of car he's driving. Some of the things I'm picky about include: a guy who doesn't wear a necklace, who doesn't use a key chain, and who ain't bald. These small details are the things you need to look past if you have a good connection with a guy. Identify what they are for you.

On the other hand, standards are kind of like the packing checklist you make before a trip; you need to make sure you have all of these things before you depart on your new relationship. This checklist must include the key things you're looking for in a partner. It's important that you're aware of them because not everyone you'll encounter, as lovely as they can be, will be a good fit for a relationship. Having standards will help you avoid wasting time and energy in a relationship that'll end up nowhere so you can save it for the right one. Some of my standards include: open mindedness, drive, ambition, intellectual curiosity, confidence, outgoingness, and great communication skills. I won't settle for any less. Remember, you can have as many standards as you wish, but you can't be too picky, or you'll miss out on great connections.

On Dates:

I'm a firm believer that one should go on as many dates as possible (as long as the suitor has some potential). Going on a first date never gets less stressful. When I was in university, my roommate and I used to get so stressed out about what to wear and what to talk about that we would sometimes start freaking out about standing them up. So we started this tradition of taking a shot of cheap brandy together before a date—if you've been on a date with me between 2014-2017, chances are I was probably tipsy. What's the worst thing that can come up from going out on a date? Worst comes to worst, the date is platonic, you both pretend you had a nice time, which you did, you both say you'll text, which you don't, and you both move on and forget about each other.

Ok. I'll tell you what's actually the worst that can happen. You go out on a date at Arbory Afloat in Melbourne with a guy named Dean from Chicago and midway through the date he starts touching your leg and telling you he wants to eat you out before you guys even had the chance to share a first kiss (there's a reason why this example is oddly specific). That's the worst. But most of the time, dates are just ok. It's ok to have a nice time and keep liking their pics on Instagram from time to time, and it's also ok to never call them back. Dating is exactly like life in general, the more you take opportunities, the more likely it is that something great will come out of it. Plus, what else do you really have to do on a Wednesday night?

On Authenticity:

We all want to present our best selves when it comes to dating, which is totally understandable. That being said, you should never try to tame yourself or avoid saying things for fear of looking too intense and making them run away. The more authentic and vulnerable you are, the more you create a safe place for the other person to be authentic and vulnerable.

When I was in university, dating was a living hell! We would play all sorts of wicked games. Texting was the worst. We would consult our friends on what to say and wait to reply to not look *too intense,* to not look *too into them.* Then, we would have to wait what seemed like years to get a text back.

Let me tell you, the only thing worse than waiting for someone to text back is waiting for your Uber after a night out at when it's negative twenty-five Celsius, and you idiotically chose to wear your mini skirt instead of your Kanuk coat because being left on read was more terrifying to you than dying of hypothermia. Never again. So, we would make ourselves cute and drop a selfie on the gram to get our crush of the month's attention. But also, to remind him that we were awesome and we had options. I was so lame and intense; I get why they all ran away.

Coming on strong about who you are with someone will not make the right person run away. Say what you want to say, double text if you want to and forget all the rules about what you should say or do. I told my ex "I love you" for the first time three dates after we met, and he didn't run away. I don't recommend doing it, it was obviously overly intense, but he stayed. Act from a place of authenticity. Games will only create unhealthy relationships where you're scared anything you do could make the relationship crumble at any point.

On People Who Are Bad for You:

Only you get to decide how much sh*t you put up with. You are in control of how you let people treat you.

On Fighting:

I have never seen my parents fight. Like, never. I don't think they never have arguments, but that they instead go downstairs and hide in the basement to do it. Kidding, I think they just never did it in front of us. But because of that, I've always found it difficult to have fights, and every time it would happen, I would think to myself "If we really loved each other we wouldn't be fighting." This is obviously wrong. I learned that arguing is normal; there's instead a thing called healthy fighting.

Fighting is inevitable, just like buying unnecessary stuff when you let yourself wander into the house decoration section of Target. Fighting can be turned into something productive or, at least, something a little bit easier to handle. You read that correctly. Making a fight productive means taking time to pause before replying to make sure you are responding and not reacting. Don't bring up things from the past, it just makes the other person feel like you've been holding a grudge against them for a while. Stay in the present.

And try to explain things by saying how you feel instead of throwing attacks. In case you need a small reminder, name calling is not productive, screaming is not productive either. Be mindful, words can't be taken back and as long as they stay, they hurt.

On a Broken Heart:

I had my heart broken so many times. I remember the first time it broke like it was yesterday. I cried the whole morning. Then my dad came into my room and told me to put it back together because my younger brother was coming back from high school for lunch. I remember the feeling, and even though my handling of the pain of a broken heart has changed (it's seriously improved), the level of pain has never gone away.

It just feels like your heart is heavy. But slowly it begin to feel lighter. At first, you're be hit with waves of grief many times a day but, after a while, those waves become fewer and further apart. Eventually, you realize that the weight has all but disappeared.

When you start seeing someone, you either break their heart, they break yours, or you stay together forever. So breakups are kind of a fatality. The pain is inevitable. Getting your heart broken isn't the end of the world. It doesn't mean all hope is gone. It means you get a second chance at creating a long-lasting relationship again. You get a second chance at creating yourself again. It's a blessing that teaches you what you care about, what moves you.

Embrace all the ups and downs in your relationships as well as your break ups. You have to fail to become the person you deserve. Heartbreak gives us the motivation to try new things for ourselves, to work on our toxic traits. Allow yourself to feel sad, it's human, but remember that sometimes you're just a heartbreak away from perfecting your glow up. Accept the grief, rebuild your heart and open it fully again, and again, and again, until you find the person you'll be annoying to for the rest of your life. No matter how dirty the breakup is, or how much it hurts, you always get through it.

I've always thought I wouldn't find someone better after a split but I did find better, every time. And if you end up not finding someone else, go get yourself that guinea pig your parents refused to buy you when you were a preteen.

I recommend unfollowing your ex on Instagram. I really mean it, unfollow him. Nothing ruins your day more than seeing your ex hanging out at your favourite restaurant with a new girl.

On When to Have Sex:

This is such an old debate. My friends and I used to have this theory that even if you liked someone and you wanted to be with them you couldn't have sex on the first date. I believed that if I had sex on the first date the guy wouldn't be interested in talking to me afterward, since he'd have gotten what he wanted. So, I'd put on my ugly underwear (the pair you usually keep for when you have your period) and purposely avoid shaving before a first date just to be sure I wouldn't be tempted to fall into bed after a first date. Well my friend, I've dated guys I tortured into not having sex for three months. Unsurprisingly, those relationships didn't go anywhere.

I did have sex on the first date with one guy I ended up being with for over a year. Having sex later on in the dating process might help, but I don't think it'll change anything in the long term. You should have sex whenever you want. I know for a fact I attach sex with emotion, which is why I can't have a one night stand without crying myself to sleep afterward (and desperately exfoliating the memory out of my body until I take off my first layer of skin the next day). But you're not obligated to be this way, nobody is obliged to be this way. It's all about respecting your boundaries and being happy with your own sex life.

On Fear of Missing Out:

Social media and online apps make dating feel like an all-you-can-eat buffet. We feel like there are endless options on who we can date, which obviously impacts commitment. I've been personally victimized by this. I would go on date then see people online who looked like an even better option. I wouldn't commit to anyone because I was scared that I would miss out on a better option elsewhere. I always thought that someone that would fit me better—always. There's actually a running gag between my friends who say that I'll probably end up being married with kids, and one day I'll tell my husband I'm going out for milk and never come back...Future husband, if you're reading this, I promise I won't say that (I don't even drink milk).

Finding someone you love and have a secure relationship with isn't always easy. In fact, It's very hard. Finding a person you can build a deep connection with is a gift. We need to stop thinking that we need to maximize the number of people we date in order to find the "best match" or "perfect match." No such things exist.

The options you see online might not suit you as well as you think, and if they do, they will still need work. If you are happy with your partner and he respects and challenges you then you've already got it all. We often buy into the stupid belief that we can find someone who is like our partner but a little extra—the extra being the thing you wish they have. Well, we're just buying into the delusion our high expectations create for us (which is picturing a cute guy on Instagram with all the personality traits we've seen in Hallmark movies). But believe me, the next best thing to your high expectations is finding someone you can grow with and who is willing to work on your relationship. If you've got that, then you've already got it all.

On Dating Apps:

Dating apps are for desperate people, but we all get desperate from time to time. Hopefully you're just not the type of desperate who pays for the premium versions. When you've been single for ages, you just get those moments when you crave attention and want to feel wanted. You download dating apps, you create a profile, you swipe left on a hundred people, then feel like it's pointless so you delete your dating apps again and the cycle continues.

Sometimes, you might swipe right on a few people you matched with, but you never make the first move and the same goes for them. Sometimes, they do make the first move but you feel like it's awkward and you stop responding. We get used to ghosting and getting ghosted.

In Quebec, everyone on dating apps is your sister's ex, your cousin, your friend from high school—it's very weird, and it makes the whole thing seem even more useless. Most of the time, dating apps don't get you anywhere. Most people on there, including myself, are just looking for a self-centered confidence boost. We want the matches because, even if we never talk to each other, they act as a compliment, which makes us feel like we won something.

Dating apps can be great, I know a few people who met their partner on there, but most of the time they don't work and that's why you shouldn't read too much into this.

Don't get frustrated because, even though there's hundreds of thousands of profiles online, you can't find anyone. Again, people are more looking for personal reassurance than something real. I think you should use dating apps as a tool to increase the mathematical chances of finding the right partner, but you shouldn't put all your eggs in the same basket.

On Making the First Move:

Where I come from in Quebec, dating is very different from anywhere else I've been in the world. For example, the season affects dating: in fall everybody is looking to find a partner to snuggle with during the cold winter months, while spring is known as the breakup season (winter has been hard and everybody is excited about getting outside again and living a life full of adventures).

Guys here hardly ever make the first move. They don't make any moves in fact. I don't know if it's the fact that marriages are not expected so they tend to be more chill about dating, but if you want something to happen here, you gotta do what you gotta do. That means letting them know you're into them first and organizing the first date, which is quite different from what I've seen elsewhere.

Living in San Francisco, I got hit on on a daily basis and it was absolutely great. I love getting hit on. Usually in Quebec, people hit on each other at social events or at bars but usually not in a casual setting, such as on the bus. So this was a totally new and exciting experience for me. It made me realize how everyone out there shouldn't be shy about making the first move. Worst comes to worst, the person is not interested or they already have a partner, but you'll never look weird (ok, if you ask them for a hug after that's kind of odd…speaking from personal experience).

I've never been hit on and thought the person was weird after, it actually always made me feel a little bit better about myself. And honestly, is there a better feeling than making someone else happy? The advice here is if you see someone you could be into, make the first move, don't lose an opportunity to make something happen.

On Finding la Crème de la Crème of Partners:

To find the best partner, you need to be the best partner.

But if I were you, I would also come and visit Canada, especially Ontario; Ryan Gosling, Ryan Reynold, Justin Bieber, Justin Trudeau,

Shawn Mendes, The Weeknd, Drake. The Great White North is actually pretty hot.

On Getting an Abortion:

When I was 19, I had an abortion. Oddly enough, even to this day, this is not a topic I've really been open about with anyone. I decided to write about my abortion anyway, as it has been the most grown-up event to date. For whatever reasons, when I started having sex, I always told myself that if I ever got pregnant at a young age, I was going to have an abortion. But I had never really imagined myself getting pregnant at such a young age. I had the misconception that since I was on the birth control pill, it couldn't happen to me. After all, this is the kind of thing you see on "16 and Pregnant" on MTV not in real life.

My situation didn't fit with my preconceived idea of a girl who becomes pregnant so young. I did not have several partners, I was responsible about contraception, and my parents had educated me on the subject. I might have forgotten a pill, but it didn't make me in any way careless about this stuff. I always had the firm idea that children were not something I was going to have until I had completed my education and was able to provide a stable environment. I think it's society's image of girls who get pregnant at such a young age that has made me unable to talk about my abortion for many years, even with my closest friends.

I remember the moment I started to suspect that I might be pregnant. It was shortly after the holidays and classes had just started again. I kept having bouts of nausea even though I was in good health. My period was late, but I didn't really panic about it until I got the nausea since I was used to having my period about every month and a half. I waited another week, living in denial, believing that pregnancy was not a possibility.

I finally had a maternity test, which turned out to be positive. I still didn't want to believe it. When I finally announced it to my boyfriend, he just said "it's your decision, but I can't live with this. My friend is waiting for me, I have to go to the gym."

After he got back from the gym, he let me know that it wasn't something he wanted and that if I told my parents about it, he wouldn't come back to visit them.

So, I decided to end the pregnancy. Yes, I realize now how horrible his reaction was and how it impacted my healing process.

The next step was to make an appointment at the hospital to confirm the results—unfortunately, it was still positive. I panicked and immediately made it clear to the nurse that I wanted to have an abortion.

Before the abortion, I attended a mandatory meeting with a social worker to make sure I was making an informed choice and that I fully understood what I was doing. Yes, I had doubts. I knew if I kept the child they would have a good life. My parents had the resources to help me and would have done it without even thinking twice. I also knew that it wouldn't stop me from continuing my education, but my life, my 20s, would be forever changed. I was not ready for that. There was also one thing. If one day I was going to have a child, I knew it wouldn't be with a guy who reacted so callously when I need support the most.

During the procedure I was sedated, but I was conscious. I remember the nurse holding my hand and offering me compliments on my nail polish while I heard the sound of the machine in the background. It sounded like I was at the dentist's office. By then, although I regretted it was too late. Then, I went back to a small rest room where I was given a little apple juice box. The only thing I remember is the colour of my slippers: white with sky blue checks, and the reason is that I kept my eyes on the ground all the way. I couldn't look up.

After my abortion, it was several months before I was able to have sex again because I was scared. And when I did, I cried. To this day, I still have remorse. Not about the decision to have an abortion. Having an abortion was the best decision of my life, though I do feel guilty about feeling that way. But I'm still haunted by the thought that it might have been my only chance to get pregnant one day.

You can hope and dream of having children, but nothing is certain. It's not guaranteed that you and your partner will be fertile. I am still haunted by the thought that maybe I missed out on my only chance to be a mom.

I find it important to talk about my abortion because it taught me two crucial things. The first is never to judge the decisions of other people in relation to situations that I have not experienced myself.

Because now I completely understand why some girls decide to keep their baby when they are so young, and now I never judge them for that. They have all my respect; they're one kind of powerful, strong women and they deserve to be seen like that by the whole darn world. The second is, there is no point in wasting your time with someone you don't see sharing your children with, if you want to have some of course. I don't mean here that you have to be 100% sure or it's worth dumping their ass, but if you can't see yourself having children with someone, if you can't see them bringing to the table the things you wish for them, it probably means you're with someone who isn't right for you and you shouldn't be with someone for the sake of killing time.

Although abortion is legal in Canada, and it hasn't really been a debate since I've been alive, (it's been a little more than three decades since Morgentaler), I still feel abortion it's stigmatised. So is getting pregnant and keeping a child at a young age. But the truth is, unless you practice sexual abstinence, which is fine, none of us is immune to a situation like this. I hope that by sharing my story, it'll help make the conversation around abortion a easier, less judgemental. I hope the next girl that ends up in a similar situation to mine feels safe enough to ask for the support she really need.

On Loving Someone:

I'm not sure if there's a right or a wrong way to love. What I'm certain of is that I've tried to love everyone I have ever dated in the best way I knew how. (Lucky for them, I got better over time). They all left with a small piece of my heart, and I hope they took it to love whomever they end up with better. I hope they've learned to create a safe and secure place for their partner to come to, a place where they both feel accepted. I hope that they've learned to show respect and openness so they cultivate trust where they allow themselves and their partner to discuss anything and everything about what's bothering them outside and inside the relationship.

I hope they've learned to step into a relationship with hope, dreaming of falling in love and creating a life filled with happiness. I hope I taught them what compassion, understanding, complicity, and partnership was like. I wish everyone could love that way. I wish everyone could be loved that way. Every time you fall in love, I hope you love in the best and kindest way you know, and that you keep learning to become a great lover.

On Settling:

You don't need to settle for anything. I strongly believed that, by the age of twenty-five, I'd be married and have kids, but age doesn't define when you should or shouldn't do things. Sure, having someone to talk to about everything is great. Especially when all of your friends are settling down or coupling up; you feel left out. But there's so much more to aspire to than being in a relationship, and this is coming from a hopeless romantic. You are smart, courageous and you can do whatever you set your mind to. You don't need anyone to make you happy or make your life better; you and only you, can do that.

You're a total babe. Don't settle for someone who just good enough. Don't settle for any less than *magic.* Keep searching until you find someone you admire, someone who makes you the best person, someone who shares your goals, your visions and your excitement, someone with whom you can be authentic and vulnerable, someone who respects you, someone who's willing to invest in the relationship and choose you everyday.

Don't settle for anything that makes you feel less than fully alive, that makes you feel like your life is anything less than perfectly imperfect. Like when you buy a perfect dress from Marshalls only to find later at home that there's a loose thread and that's why it was so cheap, but it doesn't matter because it's still the perfect dress.

Choosing a partner is the most important decision you'll ever have to make. We often hear that we don't get to choose your family, but choosing your partner is kind of the closest thing we have to it. Choosing your partner is choosing with whom you're building your new-ish family.

It feels good to find the salsa to your chips, but it feels even better when you find your guacamole (extra lime zest please).

Dear thirty-five-year-old Annie,

Hey you. It's me! I mean it's you, the younger you. I'm wondering, do you go by madame, or mademoiselle, or grand-maman now? I'm kidding. But seriously, I hope these lion's wrinkles didn't go worse, that you've become a hot soccer mom and that you're driving a SUV and not one of these horrible minivans—yuck. Above all, I hope you have and had the most fulfilling life so far and that you were able to fully recognize the person who adds to it.

I hope you ended up finding good love.

I hope you found someone that brings out the best of you. Actually, let me rephrase that, I hope you bring out the best of each other. I hope you found someone that you admire. A person that always makes you want to try a little bit harder and reach a little higher. A person you admire so much that it makes you step into the best version of yourself possible. Without pressuring you but instead because they lead by example and feel like they stand much to learn from. Without changing you but by enhancing your positive qualities and showing you all the potential you have (believe me gurl we have so much of it). Someone that believes you can succeed and help you get where you want to go, because they just know how important it is for you. A person who's selfless and wants what's best for you. I hope you're with someone whose words and actions inspire you. So much that they make you dream bigger and believe that indeed anything is really possible.

I hope you found someone who feels the exact same way about you. I hope you found someone you can build up during hard times. I hope you make them realize their true potential by believing in them head over heels. I hope you too make them better by leading with example.

I hope you found someone who's open minded and wants to make you try new things. Like the famous Pussycat dolls said: "I don't need a ring around my finger to make me feel complete."

I hope you found someone who doesn't complete you but compliments your weakness and your strengths. I hope you're both in complete awe and see something unique, extraordinary, irreplaceable and special in each other. I hope you found someone who understands you, someone you don't need to translate your soul to. I hope you're able to discuss anything and everything, calmly (the calmly is for you). I hope you found someone you love each day through the ups and the downs, the imperfections and complaints, the irritations and the short coming and the differences and decisions.

If you have, please, please, please don't let this person go. If you haven't please, please, please still don't settle for any less. You're a goddamn princess and you don't deserve any less.

Annie, xx
PS: Take care of mom and dad

MAN, I HAVE ISSUES!

Let's face it, we all have issues. No, this isn't a personal attack. This is me putting everyone in my boat so I don't feel like I'm the only troubled one out there–If we're going down, we might as well go down together!

People often say that while you're in your twenties, you don't have "real" problems. I think whoever said it was an easy decade needs to be shot right in the face...with a snowball. C'mon, I'm Canadian after all.

Being in your twenties is challenging. It comes with high expectations and great uncertainties. Society gives us thirty as a deadline for a great number of "achievements." We need to have a successful career (whatever that means), get a high paying job (which was supposed to be easy because you got a BA just like they told you to), buy a car, buy a house, get married and have children. Which means you and I have basically 5 years to accomplish e-v-e-r-y-t-h-i-n-g! Pretty stressful if you want my opinion (I know you didn't ask). I mean there are a lot of things I still don't know about taxes, or car payments, or mortgage, or budgeting, or even nurturing a plant (RIP to my last succulent). How will I ever be able to afford braces for my children? How will vacation ever feel like vacation if it's so dang expensive? I can't afford paying for an extra bag of chips at Chipotle, so how on earth will I ever be able to do all that?

Also, out of curiosity, if all of this is supposed to happen in your 20's, what's exciting about the other decades? Do you spend the years after going to your condo in Florida during winter thinking you made it and just wait until the days finally stop piling up? Have you ever watched the Florida news? That's going to be a hard no from me!

In so many ways, I get it though.

If you don't start working on some things now, you'll likely wake up at thirty-five with limited time and resources to make e-v-e-r-y-t-h-i-n-g happen, and you won't be able to make some of the hopes and dreams you had happen for yourself.

Sure, adulting is stressful. It's you against an indefinite number of days and years not knowing where to start or how to start to make e-v-e-r-y-t-h-i-n-g happen. There are no fixed plans, schedules, or goals like when we were in school. Of course, it'd be nice if someone could finally write a dummies guide titled: *Here's how to live your life for the next 60 years.* Although, it might make life quite boring. But in my opinion, the stress of adulting isn't really the heart of the problem here.

Here's another unwanted opinion of mine: the hardest part of overcoming a quarter-life crisis isn't setting out on your own unpaved path and making your dream life happen. The hardest part is believing you can actually do it. But the thing is, you have to believe you can do it, because if not you, who? Definitely not your grumpy uncle Vernon.

Like my dear friend Elle Woods said during her graduation speech in *Legally Blonde*

"You must always have faith in people, most importantly, you must always have faith in yourself".

I often talk about how I don't know exactly what I want to do, or that I haven't found my purpose. That's all I talk about actually. Deep down, I know that's just an excuse to keep myself in limbo (not that I actually enjoy it).

As I mentioned earlier, for a very long time, I was obsessed with finding my purpose.

I went and lived abroad for a while hoping that an awakening moment would happen during my long soul searching journey just like Julia Roberts in *Eat Pray Love*.

How cheesy. Of course, it never did. I came back home with more questions, still haunted by the feeling of falling behind. Except that now, I was maybe actually falling behind for real since the rest of my friends actually accomplished things while I was hanging out at the beach in Santa Cruz. *Oups!* A lack of purpose shouldn't be an excuse to not act on your own life. In fact, finding your purpose seems to me more about getting yourself out of your own head so you can just start living and learning as you go. So why don't we just do it?

I'll let you in on a secret of mine. Uncertainties aren't my greatest opponent. Adulthood isn't my greatest opponent. I am my greatest opponent. I get in my own way all the time. Here's a glimpse of my inner critic's favourite pep talks: "I'm not good enough," "I'm falling behind," "I'll never be smart enough to do it," "I'm stupid." My inner critic is my biggest bully! And quite a she-devil. I named her Margaret. I believe we all have an annoying inner voice that tells us what we can or can't do. A voice that criticizes everything you do, and just doesn't believe in you. That voice always sees the glass half empty. I called mine Margaret so I can scream "SHUT THE FU*K UP MARGARET" when she gets annoying. It feels great! You should name yours too.

At some point, we all feel stuck. Isn't that the whole point of having an existential crisis anyway? We feel stuck because the gap between our dream life and our current not-so-great life can seem too huge to cross. I believe the difference between those who can fiercely navigate their 20's and the ones who hit an iceberg and sink like the Titanic lies in a person's self-esteem and self-confidence. I am not sure if it is the lack of self-esteem or self-confidence that triggers a quarter-life crisis or if they're consequences of it. Apparently, literature also doesn't agree on the matter. A lack of confidence in our worth and our skills fuels anxiety, stress, uncertainty, questioning, and the phenomenon of comparison that leads to the crisis.

On the other hand, experiencing a quarter-life crisis can cause feelings of self-doubt that might not have been there before. It's all too easy to fall into a downward spiral of feeling uncertain and worthless when self-doubt arises. But let's all agree on something here: it's a vicious cycle either way.

If you're like me, a kid from the 90's—the glorious decade of the *Spice Girls*—you've been raised with more options, more access, more resources, and more support than any other generation in history but also, let's be honest, with way less autonomy. Which means that we know we can achieve anything (kind of), and people expect us to go out in the world and accomplish great things, but we've never learned to do anything on our own. When your parents keep you from failing, you never truly learn how to trust yourself. In fact, you learn how to always seek reassurance from others which slowly makes you afraid of uncomfortable feelings such as fear, stress, and anxiety. So, you start seeking constant reassurance from the world to tame this discomfort and with time only intensify your low confidence because you're training your brain to be afraid of being afraid (meaning you basically become always afraid of everything you'll need to face).

Most of us get stuck during our twenties because we felt like there was nothing we could do to make our life great. We are letting our low self-esteem and confidence grow into more and more fears until we feel trapped. I know for a fact I was letting fear take control over me all the time. I had so many fears. Fear of not doing enough, fear of not being up to it, fear of not living to my full potential, fear of missing opportunities, fear of failing, fear of being judged. Fear is a funny thing. Fear keeps us safe, at least in some ways. Fear used to be very handy, it kept us alive when we were living in the wild and were threatened to get killed by wolverines and polar bears on a daily basis—there was never a good time to do your nails back then! (Ok, I'm not 100% sure it was like this, I'd have to ask my First Nation ancestors). Today, fear is that thing that makes us think that if we just do one more class, one more practice, one more thing then we'll be ready, we'll be enough. Fear keeps us from failing or being hurt.

But fear keeps us from truly living—from learning, from becoming better humans. I was chained by fear, and I don't think it's presumptuous to assume that many of us are.

For most people, self-confidence is not something that is innate, but rather something that they have built. For me, it's not something I work on. I had rather spent my life doing the opposite. Kind of like Lindsay Lohan, who had a great career as a kid but spent the last decade or so ruining it. Now it was all catching up to me. Yup, maybe years of growing *issues* had finally got the best of me. And, man, believe me I have *issues*!

As I worked on my self-confidence, I realized that my performance anxiety, my perfectionism and my chronic fear of failure, were all *ugly goblins* working together to ruin my confidence like the Grinch ruining Christmas.

Let's take a look at how I worked on my confidence and all my *ugly goblins.* Working on yourself is your secret sauce to becoming a go-getter.

BECOMING THE BEYONCÉ OF SELF-CONFIDENCE

Post-graduation blues are full of self-doubts about our identity and the direction we *should* take. For most new grads, it's the amount of self-doubts piling up, and keeping them from moving forward, that create a lack of confidence. For me, my lack of confidence just comes from my personality; I'm super critical of myself. I know, being self-critical is *so Virgo* of me, but it doesn't have to be this way, one shouldn't be afraid to defy the stars!

I never understood just how much my lack of self-confidence was keeping me from living the life I wanted and just how low it truly was. Full disclosure: it was almost as low as Paris Hilton's low-rise jeans in the early 2000's. I wonder if girls back then trimmed their bikini lines only to wear jeans. *Mystère et boule de gomme!*

It all came to me one day during the holidays. My little brother made a harmless joke, so harmless that I don't even remember what it was. What I remember is being very defensive about it, so much that he replied, "Calm down, you're so sensitive.

You just don't get jokes." His reply got me thinking, a lot. He was right, I became very sensitive to jokes. Offhand comments and jokes now felt like personal attacks. Actual criticism was much, much worse. The slightest hint of negativity was all I needed to feed my bitchy inner criticism. It was giving my inner critic proof that I was indeed, never enough.

Being more aware of the problem, I slowly realized that I was constantly apologizing for anything and everything and that it was impacting how I perceived myself. Over the years, a lot of people in my circle actually called me out on the fact that I was apologizing way too much and for unnecessary reasons. Which I often reply with something like: "Sorry, I say sorry too much." But now it was just out of control, just like my eighteen-year-old self drunk on Sour Puss. I only realized how bad it was affecting me when, one day, my parents sat down with me and asked if something had happened to me.

I can't begin to imagine how hard it must have been for my parents to sit down with me to ask if I'd been assaulted. They must have thought about it for so long. They told me that they had noticed I was saying sorry for things I had no need to apologize for. They felt like I was putting myself down and making myself small, that I was essentially sorry to be me. It was raining, I was sorry. I didn't know the answer, I was sorry. They didn't have lemons at the grocery store for the Caesar salad, I was sorry. Sorry, sorry, sorry. Always sorry, like somehow everything was my fault. Thinking about this just makes me want to shake myself and scream "WAKE UP GIRL! What are you sorry for? You don't own a lemon farm in Mexico. You don't drive the food truck. You don't own the grocery store. You don't put the lemons on the shelf." That felt good.

I was the perfect stereotype of the Canadian who always apologizes. And I didn't want to prove foreigners right; I already drink more maple syrup than water. We Canadians have made saying sorry our unofficial national anthem. We seriously need to understand that apologizing when there's no reason to apologize is not being polite. We have to be careful when we do so. Apologizing when there's no reason to is making yourself small compared to others and, honestly, it makes you feel like you're a burden and that you have nothing figured out. Feeling like this just plain sucks. It's just feeding your insecurities and it's keeping you in a place of low self-confidence.

But taking things people say or do personally and saying sorry too much were not the only way in which my lack of confidence showed. I was also carrying a ton of insecurities. I wasn't feeling deserving or capable of "more" and putting myself down on a day-to-day basis (thanks Margaret).

One night, as I sat at my desk feeling really stressed over my future, not that this was any different than my usual Monday or Saturday night, but I finally had enough. About time, eh? I made a plan to become the Beyoncé of self-confidence! I'm pretty sure this is the modern-day project equivalent of building the pyramids for the Egyptians: not an easy task. I opened my computer and googled everything I could about building up self-confidence. You know…the kind of search where you have the smallest problem so you go online and end up finding out that you might have a very rare type of cancer that only 0.005% of the population survive.

From that moment on, my vision of self-confidence changed drastically.

Self-confidence isn't a term that only applies to cocky jocks, it isn't only reserved for the minor league hockey player types with scraggly playoff beards who have zero doubt they'll get drafted by the NHL (or into your bed, *yuck*). This idea of confidence is too often confused with narcissism. Self-confidence is allowing yourself to be who you are and be authentic every day. It is knowing your own values, opinions, and emotions, and being true to them in all situations. It is being vulnerable and accepting your imperfections while knowing you're still worthy. It is that powerful force that banishes your self-doubt and makes it easier to go after whatever you put your mind to.

Self-confidence is to be courageous.

Being courageous is allowing ourselves to take the first steps despite our fears and to try things we have never done before despite our fears, fears of looking silly or that things might go wrong. More than that, it's making peace with the idea of being imperfect. It's being vulnerable and authentic in relation to what you are despite what others might think.

It's showing up every day being you, without being able to predict what the impacts will be. Over time, this courage transforms into greater and greater confidence. As you take on more adventures and projects in the name of courage, you'll develop your skills, you'll see results, you'll experience success, you'll have greater confidence so having courage will become easier and easier.

Having confidence does not mean that you will not fail. You will probably fail hundreds of times. Brace yourself! But it will make you more resilient. You will see solutions where you only saw problems before. You will be more motivated to solve them because you will have confidence. It'll help you take bigger and bigger challenges and bounce back quickly when you encounter failures in your life.

Unfortunately, I don't have magic potions to boost it. I would really like to be Hermione and be able to cook something up for you, but I'm still waiting for my Hogwarts letter, sorry pumpkin.

Building your confidence won't be done overnight, nor in the time it takes to watch a TedX Talk (if only it were that easy). It will probably help you get through the day and that's pretty much it.

It also doesn't happen by subscribing to accounts that share inspirational quotes on Instagram. The same goes for those flashy books on your shelf. I know. I understand. It feels good to read and be made to believe for 5 minutes that "everything happens in due time," that "something better awaits you elsewhere," or to "stay calm, the universe has plans for you."

One sure thing is that we can't passively wait for something to suddenly change. We already do enough waiting for the FedEx guy to come with our package. We have to act. We have to put ourselves out there, build the foundation of our self-confidence, face our fears and create our lives. We have value to share with the. We can't always chicken out in life, or else we'll be stuck in an existential crisis until the end of times.

Some advice on building your self-confidence (no science here, it just worked for me):

Stop Saying You're Sorry:

Stop over apologizing. I don't want you to become a rude human being who never apologizes, that's be very un-Canadian of me. If you do something wrong, please apologize (only if you mean it). But I do want you to cut off the unnecessary apology out of your vocabulary. Saying sorry for unnecessary reasons such as asking for the waiter at the restaurant to bring you ketchup is just a way to make yourself small and inferior to others.

Whenever you can, replace *sorry* with thank you. For example, if your Lyft driver has been waiting for you for the past 5 minutes while you were trying to find your wallet, thank him for waiting instead of apologizing. By doing so, he'll definitely be less annoyed by you being late since he'll feel like he did something kind. And you'll feel less bad about yourself because you won't feel like you did something wrong. That's what is called a win-win situation.

Stop Judging:

Stop judging and criticizing yourself and stop judging and criticizing others. Low self-confidence comes from the fact that you speak to yourself negatively and these negative statements are often the result of what you imagine that others think of you.

When you have the habit of judging others, it's much easier to imagine that others are always judging you. If you think happier thoughts about others, the happier you'll be and the better you'll feel about yourself.

The most insecure people are often the people who judge the most since they like to push others down to build themselves up. Don't go there.

What I try to do is avoid judgements in my own head, but also avoid them in my conversations with my friends - aka the small talk. And it starts by avoiding gossip and minding my own business.

I realized that the more I had confidence in myself, the less I judged and this made me into a better person - the kind of person I want to be.

Identify Your Self-limiting Beliefs:

Beliefs are lens through which you see the world. They are shaped by a lot of things, by fear but also by experience, education, or our environment. Beliefs are useful, they guide us to define ourselves as worthy or worthless, loved or hated, competent or incompetent, powerful or powerless.

Self-limiting beliefs are the beliefs we have about ourselves and others that are untrue and limiting. As a result, they negatively affect our sense of self-worth and confidence.

When we feel scared, our inner mom who wants to protect us causes us to create self-limiting beliefs. And we give into them because we think they serve us by helping us avoid failure or judgement of others. But, in reality, they don't. They just limit our horizon and hold us back from taking advantage of experiences, of opportunities, of life. If you don't believe something is true or can happen, you won't do it. Therefore, it won't happen, and it'll just reinforce your limiting beliefs. For example, a long time ago people used to think that the earth was flat, and I'm pretty sure it's stopped a few people from going sailing.

Since a belief is only limiting if it stops us from doing our *thang*, we must analyze the ones we hold since they drive our attitudes, reactions and behaviors, and they definitely ruin our productivity. We need to analyze them so we can debunk them. See, unless we change our limiting beliefs, it's very unlikely that our situations will ever change—we'll always believe we can't do things, so we won't do them.

Here's some of my limiting beliefs: I'm not smart enough to study math or science, I can't do public speaking, I will never be able to start a business on my own, I'm not confident enough to ask and get what I want, and I can't publish a book because people will think I'm *très ringarde! (so tacky!)*

So, once you've identified your own self-limiting beliefs, you can identify their root causes.

Why do you believe those things? Is it because you don't believe in your own abilities? Is it because the people around you believe the same thing? Is it because you've experienced things that justify these beliefs? What is it?

After you've done that, you need to challenge these limiting beliefs. To do so, you can just use the magic tool called Google and find some counterarguments to your beliefs, or you can surround yourself with people who challenge those limiting beliefs, people who do the things you think aren't possible. Putting yourself in a new environment could be all you need. Just like we tend to be friends with people that resemble us, we also tend to surround ourselves with people who hold the same limiting beliefs as us. Why? It's comfortable, it makes us feel like we're right so we're not obligated to confront the problem. But it's important to confront our self-sabotaging thoughts, behaviors, and negatives patterns.

You can also try to forget your old beliefs by convincing yourself with an opposite, positive belief. With time your old self-limiting belief will fade away, hopefully quicker than the belly button hole I got after piercing it for a guy I had a crush on who thought it was "SoOoO hOoOoTtT!"

Just fake it until you make it - or like I like to say, believe it until you make it! Please, believe in yourself and show your mom she's wrong.

Mute Yourself:

You need to learn how to mute Margaret. Truth is, most of us lie to ourselves and others constantly when we say we don't know what we want to do with our lives. We do have plenty of ideas and dreams. Until our Margaret shows up and takes control of our narratives, saying things like, "this isn't a good idea," "what if you don't like it," "it's a waste of time anyway, you won't be able to succeed at it." If you don't tame her, you'll never be able to hear the cue your curiosity sends you, only Margaret's negativity. If you don't give energy to the BS she says, it'll pass.

Raise Your Curiosity Levels:

Don't settle. This period is about taking all the opportunities. If you want a different life, you must live differently. It starts with doing things that you would not normally do or that you have never done before.

Explore your potential instead of dreaming about it. I've been the queen of procrastinating, of sabotaging myself, of finding excuses, of complaining and feeling sorry for myself. I used to tell myself that I was going to start a pole dancing class, learn to use Photoshop and so on when I have more time, but I'd always find excuses not to start. And life always stayed the same, always meh. But one day, I started really kicking my own ass to try new things, and it's one of the best things I did. By doing something new, you discover talents and interests that you did not know you had. You discover new strengths which allow you to have even more self-confidence.

Learn new things. Developing new skills is empowering. When I started reading and taking online classes after university, I felt more empowered than ever before. Continuously learning makes you feel intelligent and capable. And believe me when I say few things feel better than feeling empowered, or when your friend's mom used you as a "good example."

Explore and say yes more. Make sure you do things that give you energy and benefit your confidence and happiness.

There are no limits to what you can do and learn. The only limits are the ones you impose on yourself to keep you in your comfort zone. They can be stretched, pushed, and broken. These are just beliefs. Remember that to learn new things, you have to do new things; the two are interrelated.

Learn and use your strengths. It will take a little effort on your part but discovering what you are good at can be a good way to quietly build your self-confidence. The best entrepreneurs in the world realize their weaknesses and seek out people to help them in areas their own experience is lacking. Now, it's important to realize that you won't excel in everything. I understand, I would also like to be good at everything. However, by recognizing what your talents are, and focusing on the development of those skills, you can become more confident even in situations that highlight your weaknesses.

Establish Goals:

Establish goals that are achievable to gain a little more self-confidence whenever a new goal is reached. Then, establish harder and harder goals. The trick is to set goals that are just a tiny bit hard, so that they motivate you enough, but don't feel unreachable. You need to be able to reach them, so you feel like you're moving forward. Setting goals related to your dreams that you can actually accomplish will boost your self-esteem and confidence because you are getting measurably closer to the person you really want to be.

To have confidence in yourself, you have to go from being a dreamer to a doer.

For a long time, I kept myself in a world of dreams and hope. I believed that, unless I did something in which I was the best, everyone would realize that I was not as good or intelligent as they believed. As painful as it may be, it is much easier to live a life of unfulfilled potential than to open yourself to the possibility that you have no potential. But you will never find that potential if you do not start taking action now to achieve your goals.

Self-confidence is built by doing things, by realizing you're actually able to do so many things and that you have agency over your own life.

PRESSURE'S ON

I struggle with performance anxiety. I can't even remember a time in recent years where I didn't. Just to be clear here, I'm not talking about sexual performance anxiety—I'll leave this one to someone else, I already have more than enough on my plate, but thanks for worrying about my sex life, you're a good friend.

Performance anxiety is basically the paralyzing fear of not having the ability to perform a task in situations where you feel like a good performance is crucial. I'm pretty sure Eminem's song *Lose Yourself is* about this, if not, the lyrics describe the feeling in an impressively accurate way: "His palms are sweaty, knees weak, arms are heavy. There's vomit on his sweater already, mom's spaghetti." But, luckily for me, my mom was never big on spaghetti.

I learned to link my performance to my worth at a very young age and it came back to haunt me years later as unwelcomed performance anxiety.

I started figure skating at 5 years old (that's late for competitive skating) and chose singles. I know they say beauty is in the eyes of the beholder or something like that, but no contest, figure skating is the most beautiful sport in the world. A perfect blend of grace and muscle strength. It pushes the limits of your body while letting everything seem easy to preserve this image of a *princess on ice*. I loved skating from the very first time my blades hit the ice (ok, almost the first time because the first time my best friend made me fall and I spent an insane amount of time crying after that, so I didn't actually enjoy it until my second practice). Skating taught me a lot, such as the importance of discipline, hard work, and sacrifice but I won't lie it also kinda screwed me up.

Figure skating is an individual sport that is based on a purely subjective. And that, my friend, is where it all goes down. You're judged on how you look, how your hair is done, how your dress looks, and how you actually perform. You're expected to land hard jumps and still look like whatever the judges define as *artistic* and *gracious*—it's a matter of taste. Since everyone you compete with, you often also practice with, nobody is really your friend.

A lot of moms don't see competition as a *fun thing*, or a "cute" passion their kids have. I like to compare skating at a competitive level to the tv show *Dance Moms*. The girls you skate with you also compete against, so it's not rare to hear other girls' moms saying pretty harsh words about how you look and your performance, words their kids would then use on the ice to belittle others.

Since it's an individual sport, you and you alone get all the prizes, attention, and admiration when you win. That's why, from a very young age, I came to believe that my appearance and my performance were directly linked to my worth. I learned that in order to win approval, I must perform well. I couldn't just do my best or work hard. Being pretty athletic, I started off really good at skating. Every competition, every appearance, became a way to seek the approval of others. So performing became more and more stressful.

Through all those years, I managed to control my performance anxiety by rehearsing a ton and visualizing. Before a competition, I stood outside the ice and I visualized myself doing my routine and succeeding, all while squeezing the life out of a little yellow stress ball (I never understood why it had a smiley face on it considering the amount of suffering this little ball had to endure). And it worked. Until it didn't anymore.

I was fourteen when I had my first panic attack. It was in French class during my oral presentation. I went in the front of the class, I started to speak, then, 30 seconds into my presentation, I froze. I couldn't speak anymore.

Why can't I speak? Why can't I remember what to say? Why am I crying? Everyone is watching me cry. Why can't I stop crying? Think of something. Say something. Everyone must think that I am an idiot. I am an idiot! Why am I not able to speak? Why am I sweating so much? What will people think of me?

"Annie-Claude, you can go sit down, take your time. We will move on to someone else and you can start again afterward."

I did not attempt to do my presentation again that day.

In fact, I never did another oral presentation in my life. I used my public panic attack as an excuse to get exempted from them. I feel ashamed of this now, but back then it felt like quite a victory. Exactly like that one time at summer camp when I told my monitor I couldn't wash the dishes since I was allergic to dish soap. I never washed the dishes that summer and still won the prize for the best camper. Today I feel pretty bad for my best friend who had to cover up my lie and ended up doing the dishes all summer when it was supposed to be my turn. What a sneaky kid.

From that moment on, every time I had an exam during that class, my teacher came to place a small sheet on my desk that said, "I am good, I am beautiful, I am capable!" Which is a sentence I now tell myself when I need to do something that triggers my anxiety.

That experience has come to haunt me though. Every time I have had to do an oral presentation since then, the memory of my panic attack has come back to me. And my performance anxiety only continued to grow over the years. My performance anxiety is triggered by some specific situations: presentations, exams, and job interviews—the last one makes adulting a little harder.

It's not just stress! I know, it's normal to be stressed before certain situations. But it is not normal to cry, to have blackouts, to feel scared and unworthy, to break out in a cold sweat. This is not simple stress, it is full-on performance anxiety. And unlike what your uncle Vernon—who grew up on a farm and who knows how to be a real man—says, performance anxiety is a real thing.

Often, when I'm faced with situations where I feel like I am being assessed or where I am at the mercy of others' judgement, my anxiety returns. Sometimes it's so bad that I can't accomplish tasks. I can't do this oral presentation. I can't make this important phone call. I can't do this job interview. Because all I keep repeating in my head is that I'll fail, and then everyone is going to think I'm inadequate or incompetent so I'm going to die—while hyperventilating, of course.

The degree of my anxiety depends on the situation and on my perception of the worst-case scenario. It also depends on the importance I attach to the situation. It starts with my desire to succeed or, if you prefer, my fear of failing. I'm afraid of looking incompetent, of making a fool of myself so I put unimaginable pressure on myself to do well.

Mainly, everything depends on the judgement of others: how they see me, what they will think or say about me if I fail. It's pretty sad to think I get performance anxiety over the perception that some strangers have of me and my life considering that they don't really care about my happiness or me for that matter.

For a long time, I tried to avoid all the situations where I was experiencing stress. But I knew I couldn't go on like that anymore, because those same situations were the ones that would allow me to move forward, grow, and thrive.

What helps me to go on despite my anxiety is a meditation technique that I discovered: the noting technique. Yup, surprisingly it's not just having someone tell me to relax, who knew?

Noting is about examining your thoughts and giving a name to what you're thinking or feeling—happy, angry, anxious—and acknowledging those thoughts and feelings for what they are. It's about separating yourself from your thoughts and emotions; it's about realizing that you are not them, which makes you feel like you have more control over them—especially the negative thoughts.

The noting technique allows me to get out of this vicious cycle of negative thinking more quickly. To avoid the spiral of "What if this or that happens?" This doesn't look like the stereotypical version of self-reflection i.e., sunrise meditation while burning scented candles or incense yearly spiritual retreats in India (definitely not planning on doing this part of *Eat Pray Love*).

I just do it casually during the day whenever I feel anxious or have a negative thought about myself or a situation. It means accepting and allowing a feeling or a thought to come and go when it presents itself in your day that might have a negative effect without assigning shame or guilt to it. Every emotion and thought is allowed. The trick is to not react to them or take them too seriously. This is what makes us feel overwhelmed. Simply acknowledge anxious or negative thoughts for what they are—speculations about the future coming straight out of your anxiety or your fear—not reality.

For example, if I'm about to do something and start hyperventilating and I catch myself thinking "What if I do this, FAIL, AND THEN DIE..." I take a second to acknowledge that it's only an anxious thought, an anxious feeling, nothing more, and I miraculously avoid a cycle of worrying, overthinking, and paralysis. Almost as good as turning water into wine, eh? I truly hope I don't sound like a hippie straight out of Woodstock right now. The only type of hippie I want to be is the one wearing floral cropped tops and speaking exclusively in ABBA lyrics.

Next time you start feeling anxious, be a *Mamma Mia!* hippie like me: take a deep breath, close your eyes, notice the emotion inside you or the thoughts galloping in your brain—frustration, anger, fear, anxiety whatever it is. Acknowledge that this emotion or thought is not "reality," it's just a feeling or a thought that will pass. Sit with it for a moment, acknowledge it, then let it go. Pass it out of your system. If you catch yourself asking "what if I fail," ask instead "what if I succeed." Proceed with less anxiety.

Of course, there are still times when the anxiety is too great, and I am unable to face certain situations, but this happens less often since I am now able to minimize the feelings that trigger my anxiety before it gets out of control. But being able to recognize that the feelings that go through my body and my mind are just the results of my anxiety and not an actual threat just really work like magic.

Anxiety doesn't define us as humans, and neither does our performance. We might want to perform well, but there's no *should*, *have*, or *must* to it. And performance anxiety or not, you'll be way nicer to yourself if you take those words out of your vocabulary too, it is an unnecessary pressure to put on yourself.

PERFECTIONISM: THE ENEMY OF EVERYTHING THAT COULD BE GREAT

Another issue of mine that kept me from going after the life I wanted is that I'm a perfectionist. Sounds familiar?

Most people believe that perfectionism is this really great thing that people who have high standards and who are insanely efficient, organized, meticulous and always prepared for the worst-case scenario have.

I even bet you my student loan that you've once been *zeee* most original person on earth and used it as your "greatest weakness" during a job interview (no shame, we all did it). I hope, on behalf of all the recruiters out there, that including in my book how *shitty* it is to be a perfectionist, it will make you a little bit more original at your next interview, or perhaps even honest about your weakness, who knows? I once said in an interview that the last thing my friends would tell them is that I'm a punctual person, since I'm always late—I still got the job!

On a side note, Quebec has way too many jobs and not enough workers, so I wouldn't really take all of my advice if I were you. Or if you do, please just don't blame me for your unemployment.

Based on this belief, perfectionism sounds great. But, even if sometimes it can be a great source of drive, most of the time it's just getting in your way of doing anything worth doing.

If perfectionists are some sort of supernatural human being who achieve great things, fear is their kryptonite. Their high expectations and need to be excellent are rooted in fears; it isn't so much that they love investing in details, they're afraid of what will happen if they don't produce something *perfect*. It's plain old fear. Fear of failure; fear of rejection; fear of negative judgement. It is selfish. It is all about you and your needs to feel *perfect* and not the goodwill of doing something for others.

In fact, it sucks, right?

To some degree, we're all perfectionists. We'll strive for greatness and want to give ourselves the life we dream of, so we tend to be critical, put in a lot of work and are scared when we don't know the outcome. But if our standards are too high, we're setting ourselves up for failure.

The demon behind perfectionism is a critical inner voice.

As far back as I can remember, I've always wanted to be *perfect*. I imagined myself growing up to be Rory Gilmore (this is my book, I have the right to make references to Gilmore Girls or any TV show as much as I please). Rory is passionate, intellectually curious, creative, funny, and pretty without trying. This was my idea of *perfect* as a kid, and that's how I wanted to be. I used Rory as an excuse to create high expectations for myself. I'd tell myself things like if I get 100% on my test, it'll mean I'm smart like Rory, if I get under this mark, it'll mean I'm stupid. Of course, my vision of "perfection" changed with time. What didn't change is my high expectations and my need to hide behind my perfectionism because I cling to the idea that if I do everything correctly, it will minimize the pain. I will avoid failure and judgement. If I'm *perfect*, everybody will just have to love me, right? But, just like the chicken pox, failure and judgement can't be avoided. Unless you buy yourself an island and quarantine there until you die, which sounds even worse than not being loved by someone who doesn't really care about you or failing at trying something you end up learning from.

Growing up, my overprotective parents also made sure I didn't fail at most things, and I was *ok-ish* enough at everything to manage being average effortlessly.

That's how I turned out 25 years old, scared as hell to fail (looking at your bill after bringing your 2000' Pontiac Sunfire to the garage, kind of scared). And with high time low confidence: the more you go without failing, the less you get to know your own abilities and the more failure can actually hurt your ego, and the more and more your confidence drops.

Failure is scary because it's difficult to process. We get caught in the thoughts that maybe it means we're a bad person or we're flawed. So, we don't want to face criticism from ourselves and from others. We don't want people to see us as flawed, because all we praised online is *perfection*. So something must be wrong with us if we aren't perfect. I used to have such a fear of what people would think of me, like they could hurt me, so I feel like I needed protection. And avoiding failure at all cost was the only way to protect myself. Back in high school, I used to care so much about what people think of me that I spend my time in high school trying to avoid wearing the same thing for a month. Who does that? (I'm aware of how privileged that sounds.)

Trying to be *perfect* has always had a negative impact on my life. When I think about it with hindsight, I often kept myself from trying new things or playing games with my friends because I put myself under pressure to be *perfect* before I even started. I would rather do nothing than risk not being the best at something. So, for a very long time, I only did things I was sure I would succeed at. I was living in my comfort zone and its limits were closing in on me a little more every day.

I avoided failing and comforted myself that it was better to fail because I didn't try things rather than failing at something I gave an honest try. It was easier to tell myself that I had the abilities to make e-v-e-r-y-t-h-i-n-g happen, just as well as the other, when I decided to try - that's kind of ridiculous. It was easier to stay in a never achieving anything state, than facing the fact that maybe I wasn't naturally good at things and needed to put the work in. I struggled with a fixed mindset, and felt like every failure would just define how bad I was. This is how I "protect" myself from my inner critic and from others perceptions of me. That's why I was so obsessed with being *perfect* and doing things *perfectly.*

It's a little ridiculous to feel like you need to be the best at badminton to play with your friends. But it was the case for pretty much everything. I kept thinking, "But what if I'm bad?" "What will people think about me?" Before I started taking salsa dance classes, I showed up a few times to the beginner classes, but couldn't get myself to go inside. So I kept going and walking around the block until I was late. Then I went back home, angry at myself. It took me two or three weeks of walking around the block to gather the courage to go to my first class. It was a blast. I sucked, but I had so much fun. I kept taking classes and got better and came to enjoy it more and more. I'm definitely not a great dancer but, one day, I'm sure my hips will move like Shakira in that "Whenever, Whenever" video clip. Just watch me.

I had difficulty developing my self-confidence because I always set unrealistic expectations and goals that I was never able to crush. So, I started talking to myself negatively. This was the worst thing I could do and the number one thing I'm still practicing stopping myself from doing.

If I didn't succeed according to my standards of perfection, I would say to myself that I was not good enough, not competent enough, not intelligent enough, not beautiful enough, never enough. Perfectionism is not a behaviour. It's an inner critic that marries your identity with your achievements or performance.

At the worst of my perfectionism behavior, I could not delegate and work in a team because I couldn't take the risk that someone else would produce something *imperfect* that would have an impact on me. This is totally silly considering that one of the strengths of the most successful people is that they are able to recognize their weaknesses and turn to other people more competent in this field to help them. We all need each other at the end of the day.

At some point during university, I had no choice but to face the problem directly. I was no longer able to study. I was paralyzed. I couldn't even open my textbooks; what if, when I opened the book, I couldn't understand the concepts, what if I couldn't remember exactly, word-for-word, everything I was about to read? I had no choice. I was in desperate need of a therapist. I know, you probably knew that from the beginning of this chapter.

After crying for the full hour of my first session, thanks to talking therapy and cognitive behavioral therapy, things have gotten better (unlucky me, I have no excuse for not studying anymore). If there's one thing I learned about therapy that you need to know, it is to always wear waterproof mascara. Even better, just don't wear any mascara. Otherwise, you might go to the grocery store afterward and only realize your face is a mess 3 hours later when you get back to your apartment. Although, this style of "makeup" does, surprisingly, make people way nicer to you. Not sure if it's out of empathy or some weird kink.

The game changer for me was realizing that my personal value is not determined entirely by my performance and my success. I wasn't worthless even if I did something *good* instead of *perfect*. But, perhaps, my personal value would be better determined by the efforts and the intentions behind what I do. Or by my progress instead of the number of times I get things right. One sure thing is we feel a greater sense of worthiness if we spend our time focusing on delivering good outcomes and helping other people rather than "looking good" or "being the best".

I asked myself these questions: Why is my performance so important to me? Why is it so important that I do everything perfectly? What will be good enough? Why is the judgement of others so important to me? Why is it more important to live for others than to live for myself?

Chasing perfection is chasing the impossible. Perfect doesn't exist. We're just chasing an imaginary destination that never has, and never will exist. You might have a better chance of reaching Narnia (honestly, good luck with that too). It is impossible to impress everyone since everyone has a different idea of what perfection is. It is hard to admit, but no matter how hard you try, you will never get everyone's approval. If you wait until you have mastered something perfectly or are yourself perfect, you'll never put yourself and your work out there, you'll never do anything.

You should try to be the best person you can be for yourself according to your dreams, goals, and ambitions. To be that person, you have to try new things and learn new things that inevitably come with failures. What others think about what you are doing should have very little impact. You should only worry about the opinions of the people you know and care about and let go of the opinions of others.

If it's the opinions of people you know and respect that scare you, you should really examine your relationships.

And I hate to say it, but people don't care that much about what you and I do. In fact, they don't care at all! People are busy. Busy doing their own thing, living their own life and fixing up their own mistakes. They don't have time to look for all your flaws. That doesn't mean they won't judge you, they might. But their thoughts about you will go away as fast as they came. Unless, like me, you're from a small town. Then yes, people will talk about you for a very long time, what else do they have to do? There's one festival a year in the village, high speed internet isn't at its finest yet, and there's like only one cute guy to lurk.

Dita Von Teese, said it best, "You can be the ripest, juiciest peach in the world, and there's still going to be somebody who hates peaches."

So, chasing perfection is a lost cause anyway!

Funny thing is, the first thing I learned at five when I started skating was actually to fail. We're told that at one point or another, we're going to fail. That's the price to pay for mastering difficult jumps and spins. We're also told that there's a good way to fall when you fail. You want to avoid putting your hands down, or failing on your hips. You always go for the butt. If you go for the butt, you can keep going without problem. You can get up and keep practicing; you can get up and finish you solo and still win. Although I learned how to *fail* at skating, I didn't learn how to *fail* in life.

Every failure has a meaning. Perhaps the way to look at failure is like this. It's either not the right thing for us or the right time. Maybe there's something better for us to come. Maybe it's experiential learning. Maybe failure is just a lesson. A piece of knowledge we take with us to do better next time. Our best chance to succeed next time. If there's one thing I'm sure of is that failing is the only way to achieve anything. It's the needle on or compass that redirect us to the direction we need to go, or the place where we need to double down.

When it comes to facing your fear, you basically have two choices: be hurt by what you or others think of you when you show up with *imperfect* or being hurt by not knowing if you could have made e-v-e-r-y-t-h-i-n-g you wanted for yourself and your life happened. I'd say the first one is way less scary.

Truth be told, there's a lot of things that can't be learned or improved unless we try, do and fail. That's why the people who failed the most, are also the one experiencing the most success and happiness out of life. Failing is the only way to know what's our real level of greatness. The one that'll make us happy and content with ourselves, the one we actually want to strive for.

So, you need to face your fear, or if you prefer, you need to move forwards even if you have fears. One thing that I've personally learned from giving into fears, is the more you let them control you, the more they'll take over you. The more of them you'll have and the more paralyze you'll become. A way to approach and tame your fear of failure is focusing on improvement and learning you're much less likely to fail since you weren't seeking success as an outcome to start with.

We need to learn to love ourselves and not try to keep up with unrelenting standards of society that are based on some random idea of excellence that we called our own. We're beautiful, we're talented, and we have the world on our plate! My teacher has been right all along.

As a recovering perfectionist, here's my advice: be self-aware, identify your self-limiting beliefs, and develop a growth mindset.

Be Self-Aware:

Growing up, our high expectations serve us. We were rewarded for our achievements, for our good grades, for being on the top charts or percentiles, so it motivated us to create higher and higher expectations for ourselves, increasing the need to perform more perfectly the next time. But, at one point in life, our high expectations will likely stop serving us. If the fear of putting something out in the world that doesn't meet your highest standards paralyzes you, then you know you need to change something.

If your standards are too high, shift them to something more manageable. Not because you can't do bigger things, but because you'll feel better knowing you've reached and surpassed them once in a while. Ask yourself what would be good enough and just aim for that.

Make space in your life for the "not perfect." See what happens when you stop obsessing over every little detail. You will likely realize that mistakes aren't the end of the world.

We are all imperfect, that's the point of being a living and breathing human being.

Identify your self-limiting beliefs:

Beliefs can be seen as the lens through which you can see the world. It's what we believe to be real. They are shaped by a lot of things from fear but also from experience, education or our environment.

Beliefs are useful, they guide us to define ourselves as worthy or worthless, loved or hated, competent or incompetent, powerful or powerless, you get the drill!

Self-limiting beliefs are the beliefs we have about ourselves, others or things that are untrue and limiting - as a result, they negatively affect our sense of self-worth and confidence.

When you feel scared, your inner b*tch, Margaret in my case, creates self-limiting beliefs. We think they serve us, by helping us avoid failure or judgement of others or any excuse we can think of, but in reality, they don't. They just limit our horizon and hold us back from taking advantage of experiences, of opportunities, of life, by doing the things we want to do. Because if you don't believe something is true or can happen, you won't do it; therefore, it won't happen, and it'll just reinforce your limiting beliefs.

For example, a long time ago people used to think that the earth was flat, and I'm pretty sure it's stopped a few people from going sailing.

Since a belief is only limiting if it stops us from doing our *thang*, we must analyze the ones we hold since they drive our attitudes, reactions and behaviors, and they definitely ruin our productivity. We need to analyze them so we can after that debunk them. See, unless we change our limiting beliefs, it's very unlikely that our situations will ever change - we'll always believe you can't do things, so we won't do them, so it won't happen, so we'll believe it more.

Here's some of my limiting beliefs: I'm not smart enough to study math or science, I can't do public speaking, I will never be able to start a business on my own, I'm not confident enough to ask and get what I want or I can't publish a book because people will think I'm very *très ringarde! (tacky!)*

So, once you've identified your own self-limiting beliefs, you can identify their root causes. Why do you believe those things? Is it because you don't believe in your own abilities? Is it because the people around you believe the same thing? Is it because you've experienced things that justify these beliefs? What is it Margaret?

After you've done that, you need to make Margaret shut up, or if you prefer, you need to challenge these limiting beliefs. To do so, you can just use the magic tool called Google and find some counterarguments to your belief, or surround yourself with people who challenge those limiting beliefs or people who do the things you think aren't possible. The people who embody the belief you're trying to switch. Putting yourself in a new environment could be all you need. Just like we tend to be friends with people that resemble us, we also tend to surround ourselves with people who hold the same limiting beliefs as us. Why? It's comfortable - it makes us feel like we're right so we're not obligated to confront the problem. But sometimes comfort, reinforce our self-sabotaging thoughts, behaviors, and negatives patterns. You can also try to forget your old belief by always convincing yourself with an opposite, positive belief. With time your old self-limiting belief will fade away, hopefully quicker than the belly button hole I got after piercing it for a guy I had a crush on who thought it was "SoOoO hOoOoTtT!", I'll forever be scared.

Just fake it until you make it - or like I like to say, believe it until you make it! Please, believe in yourself and show Margaret she's wrong.

Develop a Growth Mindset:

It all starts with the right mindset: if you are chained in fears, you need to fix your mindset. I also know these types of things are easier said than done. Exactly like getting told to not feeling sad after a break up since, according to your uncle Vernon, there's plenty of fish in the ocean. But that doesn't mean it can't be done. In fact, if an average basic white girl like me can do it, anyone can do it.

I know you don't think you need a definition, but I'll give you one anyways: a mindset can be defined as the way we think, and it's the single most important thing that affects our behaviour. Everyone has a mindset: you, your mom, your brother, your friend, your partner and maybe your dog too, and they're all different. Everyone however has a mixture of what we call a growth mindset and a fixed mindset. People with a predominant growth mindset can show a fixed mindset in some areas, while the one with a fixed mindset can have a growth mindset in some part of their lives. But we usually tend to lean more into one than the other.

I like to think about the people with a growth mindset as the learners and the ones with a fixed mindset as the non-learners.

If you believe that your abilities, talents and intelligence can be developed through hard work, good strategies and other people's advice: congrats, you have a growth mindset! If you believe that you're either naturally talented, or intelligent, or not. If a failure makes you doubt your own abilities, if you think that talent alone creates success, or if you lose interest when a task gets hard: congrats, you have a fixed mindset and are in the need of an intervention. Luckily, I'm about to give you one for free.

People who have low self-esteem or confidence are often the one stuck with a fixed mindset. When you believe you can't do things, or are unsure you have the abilities to succeed, you tend to avoid challenges, experiences and risk. You don't see the point in trying, persevering or finding solutions, so you don't. Ultimately, you do everything to prove yourself that indeed you're right; you can't do anything.

When you believe a mistake or a limit in your skills or knowledge is synonymous with being a failure instead of an opportunity to learn and outgrow yourself. So, you spend time trying to hide your flaws (since you think there's nothing you can't do about them) hoping you won't be judged. When you aren't putting in the work, you aren't achieving anything worth feeling proud of—talented or not.

This mindset is an obstacle to achieving great things and stretching yourself into a better, more capable, and more knowledgeable human being. It's important to realize a fixed mindset is limiting—you can't become more than you already are. For all these reasons, it's crushing your confidence since you're letting mistakes, failures, criticism and the unknown define your worth.

A few ways to help build a growth mindset is by replacing the "failing" with "learning" in vocabulary or changing the *can't*, with *can't yet,* the *I don't know*, which *I don't know yet*. Just adding the *yet* to the things, you haven't learned, do, or archived, gives you so much room for improvement and growth. It's like having this beautiful plant that you keep in a small pot, by just putting it in a bigger one, it would realize it could grow, and eventually will, it'll expand to be a magnificent plant worthy of your favourite home decor Pinterest board.

Mindset is everything, really. Remember that you're not doomed to suck at things you don't know or aren't good at, *yet*. You're never stuck where you are. It isn't the smartest or the most talented individuals who end up thriving the most, but rather the one who showed up, setbacks after setback, to learn and become.

Have Compassion for Yourself:

Now, I know I've talked about these issues in separate ways, but they are all deeply connected with each other and they all impact your ability to take action over your life. They'll be solved by one little trick...

The secret of self-confidence doesn't only hide in building it by accomplishing hard things and pushing your limits.

A big part of being confident is about developing a growth mindset that gives you authentic confidence. Which is partly the feelings you hold towards yourself and how you think other people value you or feel towards you, your abilities, and your qualities.

You can't make your worries go away completely by hustling, trying harder and doing better. Whoever said that to you was lying. Confidence is not about how much you achieve and how good you become (although I admit, it helps), but about your ability to be compassionate toward your weakness, your mistakes and failures. If you can't show yourself compassion, you'll only end up hiding behind more and more empty achievements while still struggling with the same issue: lack of confidence, performance anxiety, perfectionism and fear of failure.

You'll end up being living proof of the duck syndrome analogy: when we see ducks glide across the surface of a pond it looks graceful and effortless, but in reality, its little feet are paddling furiously under the water. What I'm trying to say is that your accomplishments and your success will look good on the outside but on the inside. On the inside you'll consistently be anxious and exhausted, wishing for better. You can't depend on your outward achievements, on outside approval, or on praise to value yourself. By doing so, you'll only let yourself go up and down depending on external circumstances. Every little negative comment, mistake, or failure will send you down the cliff again!

For a very long time, I tried to keep my self-confidence high by looking around and sizing up my progress versus my peers. During my academic years, I would look at the median grade and would only be kind to myself if I was above it or had the highest score. It was a horrible way of treating myself. Constant comparison just triggers your stress and it always feels like you're being attacked, like you're always wrong. It triggers your bitchy inner critic, and God knows how good it is at taking us down.

The best cure for low self-confidence is understanding where you are right now and embracing whatever thoughts, emotions and reactions you have with a nonjudgmental awareness. It's called self-compassion. My definition of self-compassion is being kind and understanding when you confront failures. It's watching the way I talk to myself, avoiding words like *always*, *should*, and *never* that only result in more negative thoughts.

It's avoiding the use of failure and mistakes to qualify my entire existence; I'm not a failure because I failed. Failure is only a situational slip-up. It's ok to feel how you feel when you fail. What's not ok is judging yourself harshly for learning. We need to stop constantly belittling ourselves for things we don't know yet or for the things we do wrong. I believe nobody goes through life without being wrong or making mistakes. No one knows it all. Not even your mom, though she tries to make you believe she does.

Responding to imperfect performance, and failure, and mistakes with self-compassion rather than self-criticism will make all of the above less scary.

No matter how messy your life is at the moment or how badly you mess up, the way you talk to yourself will define how you feel about yourself. It will define your motivation, and it will define your actions. Be ambitious and dream big but remember you don't have to know or be good at everything to be good enough. Good enough is more than enough. Showing up is more than enough. Praise yourself for the place you're in right now and the things you are already doing and have done.

HOW MANY LIKES DOES IT TAKE TO BE HAPPY?

Instagram ruined my life.

The impact of Instagram on my life is, without a doubt, huge. The feeling of inadequacy it causes in me is even more huge. It constantly makes me so anxious about who I am and what I'm worth. It makes me second-guess myself on a daily basis. What is wrong with me? Am I the only one who's not hanging out on a yacht in the Greek islands eating baba ganoush and drinking Aperol Spritzes on a Monday afternoon?!

Theodore Roosevelt said that "comparison is the thief of joy." Instagram is undeniable proof that he was right. Put out an APB because my joy has been stolen.

How are we supposed to avoid comparing ourselves, to feel good about ourselves, when we're never more than one page-refresh away from seeing someone somewhere doing something better than us, over and over again?

I remember a time when Instagram was just fun. When people would post random pictures of what they were doing. When they added some terrible quality filters to silly selfies. When likes were exciting (but not addictive) and we felt absolutely fabulous if we got 11 likes. When we were all just enjoying ourselves. Or when Facebook wasn't just a news feed of disinformation and random conspiracy theories. Can someone please tell me how we ended up here? I'd do anything to go back. I know it was only like 8 years ago, but I like being dramatic.

If you can manage to be active on social media and still feel good about yourself, this chapter might be useless to you. You probably already know what your goals are and have your own definitions of success and happiness, which we should all have. And perhaps you're also good at not comparing yourself to others. But let's be real, does a person like that actually exist?

I'm addicted to my phone. Correction: I'm addicted to Instagram and LinkedIn (I'm a nerd), but who can really blame me?

It's so easy to get hooked on platforms that provide access to other people's lives almost in real-time, especially since we carry them all day in our back pocket. I'm so hooked that I carry my phone around in my hand all day. Some nights, I even scroll the night away, fighting to stay awake to see more while my phone slips closer and closer to my face. The apps are always there, just waiting for me. I constantly need to increase my data plan, which costs me a fortune every month. Thanks, Canada, for having some of the highest wireless prices in the world! I really like struggling to decide if I should get milk or data this month!

Wondering what a day in the life of a phone addict looks like? Probably just like yours!

I wake up in the morning and the first thing I do is stretch my arm to grab my iPhone to look at what I missed during the night. I wait in line at my local coffee shop for my oat-milk chai latte, I open LinkedIn, and I scroll my endless feed. I'm on a break from work, I open Instagram and devour my "stories", aka other people's "life highlights." I wait at the doctor's office and go on Snapchat to see if my friends have sent me anything fun.

The worst thing is, social media has transformed me into a creep.

I lurk every story, every post, all day long. I mean, I didn't intend to know that your uncle's sister-in-law's new dog is lactose intolerant. Still, I know this very disturbing fact. Thank you all for oversharing!

Sometimes, I even go out on a date pretending I'm interested in knowing more about the guy while the truth is that I spent two hours before looking him up online. So, basically, I find him boring because he's not telling me anything new. I know the guy was born in Toronto, he's the third child of a family of four and his parents got divorced when he was six. He moved with his mom to Calgary when he was nine. He graduated from UBC in mechanical engineering, where he met his first girlfriend, who he broke up with to go get life experience on a long backpacking trip in South America. But I let him talk, testing him to see if will slip a lie somewhere into his very well-prepared pitch to get a second date.

And, of course, I'm also analyzing if his attitude matches his astrological sign. I told you, I'm a creep. Or, as I like to see it, a modern-day Sherlock Holmes. On a better note, it might be a good thing to reduce the probability of ending up on a date with a psychopath. Although, I don't think anyone suspected Ted Bundy.

Honestly, that's just a random example straight out of my imagination; I never actually get that far. I would never go out on a date with a guy who cheers for the Leafs or the Flames.

The amount of content I consume in a day is scary.

If you want to give yourself a heart attack, I advise you to take a look at your "screen time" on your iPhone.

"Screen time" lets you see how you use your time on your phone. The data about my time online is a real horror scene. Let me share some of them with you. I open my cell phone an average of seventy-eight times a day. Directly after opening my cell phone I usually consult Instagram. I spend an average of two hours a day staring at my phone screen and social media is the app category I use the most. At least the second category of app I use the most is the Reading and Reference category, thanks to Audible, there's still hope with me.

Looking at those stats got me thinking: *"Wow! I guess that's why I never have time to do the laundry. Oops!"*

Seriously, I swear it feels like I only open my phone for two minutes but then, twenty-five minutes of my time is gone–forever!

How can I consume so much social media content and not be deeply affected by what I see? Mission: Impossible. And most of this content is as empty in useful information as a Boston Maple Cream from Timmies is in nutritional value.

I think there are four main problems with social media: FOMO, burnout, comparison, and the focus on perfectly curated lives.

FROM FEED ILLUSIONS TO FOMO

Let's start with the fear of missing out.

As a millennial and an inspiring quarter-life crisis survivor, I wonder if I would have ever struggled with FOMO if social media didn't exist. I'm not only talking about the fear of missing out on things my "friends" on the internet are doing, but more about the feeling of missing out on life. The feeling of missing out on the pleasure, success, or fulfillment that we think everybody else is having (they don't). At the end of the day, it feels like we're losing at life if we miss out.

It doesn't take much to understand how social media creates FOMO:

- Instagram: Your "friend" is now a successful fashion blogger!
- Facebook: Your "friend" is having a girl!
- Pinterest: Your "friend" just bought a house and the decoration is on fleek
- LinkedIn: Your "friend" got a promotion in the AI industry! (insert some geek position name here)

The constant stream of notifications makes me wonder if everyone has a perfect life except me. It gets me right the stomach every time: the anxiety and the competitive thoughts. Why am I not a fashion blogger? Why am I not pregnant? Why am I still sleeping on an air mattress? Yes, you read that right, I don't even own a bed! The answer might be as simple as: I don't want any of these things ever. Or I just don't want them now!

Most of the time, my online friends' accomplishments don't seem all that attractive to me. I mean, there's nothing I want less right now than to feel the weight of a mortgage on my shoulders. Still, I feel like rubbish that I haven't accomplished these things. I feel like maybe, just maybe, I'm missing out on the best possible version of life? Maybe, just maybe, I'm doing life wrong? Maybe my goals aren't the right ones, the ones we're supposed to reach if we want to live the ideal life? Maybe I should be on the same path as the people I follow, pursuing the same accomplishments and the same life. Maybe they're the ones who have it all figured out.

When you're in an existential crisis, you're basically struggling with finding meaning, purpose and a sense of belonging in your life. Being confronted all the time by other people's accomplishments and happiness—no doubt embellished and polished off by a filter—makes you second-guess your own life's direction all the time! It makes you struggle with having one goal to start with, since everyone seems like they're already so far ahead of you. It just drags you deeper in the hole. I swear, friend, there's nothing wrong with the way you want to live your life if it makes you happy, even if it's different from the one you're bombarded by on your phone. We need to stop thinking other people's success has something to do with ours. It just doesn't.

Social media makes you forget that not everybody is reaching new milestones all the time or even trying to reach for them. For a pretty large chunk of people, most days are plain and ordinary, just like ours.

It's ok not to have a life just like the people you see on social media. There's no one-size-fits all life or set of milestones, we're all on different paths, doing different things. And for the record, nobody actually has the life of people on social media. We all play the game of embellishing and we're all making each other feel bad with our lies.

Even if you did achieve everything everybody else is doing would you be happier? I don't think so. I learned not long ago that we sometimes need to be careful what we wish for. For years, I looked at people's lives and thought, "Wow, I wish I could live abroad too." I thought it was such a cool accomplishment, and I wanted it so much. Then it happened to me. Yeah! I was finally living the sweet international life in California. What I didn't expect was that living abroad is quite lonely, and everybody else back home is busy living life without you. Sometimes, you're just surrounded by people who don't get you, your culture, your values, your morals, or your language and it's hard. Of course, being abroad makes me happy. It's actually one of the best things that ever happened to me. Deep down I wish I was able to live abroad for the rest of my days. I guess what I'm trying to say is that we might be tempted to pursue a specific kind of life because of how impressive we think it is or how it might look to other people. But, if it isn't true to you, you'll end up pretty miserable. Whether it's getting your master's, starting a business, getting promoted to a manager position, these achievements all come with a downside, so be sure you're truly doing it for you.

Perhaps the only life you and I are actually missing out on is the life we're truly meant to live. Trying to achieve what everybody else is doing on social media only distracts us from figuring out what we really want. Anyways, trying to keep up is pretty tiring.

INSTA-ANXIETY AND SOCIAL BURNOUT

Are you feeling a social media burnout yet? I certainly am.

Everybody's social media account is telling me to work out every day, eat healthier, buy local only, home cook more, find a side hustle, have time for Sunday brunch with friends, find new passions, learn new languages, start an ecom company…the list goes on. I feel like I'm always rushing to optimize my time to create a life that'll be social media perfect. A life that'll be good enough compared to the ones of all these influencers. There's just not enough time to do everything so, inevitably, I end up feeling like I'm failing at something, or everything.

It's overwhelming.

Everybody is telling me what I should care about. Advocate for climate change, feminism, animal cruelty, child labor, human rights in developing countries, worker rights in the gaming industry. They're all noble causes, and they all deserve attention. I just don't have enough time and energy to invest in all of them enough to make a significant difference, so I feel shitty.

It's overwhelming.

Even self-care is work now. You need to do productive self-care, which means reading self-development books, doing yoga everyday, meditating for 15 minutes every morning, taking a daily walk, journaling, setting goals for the upcoming year, doing face masks every week, exfoliating three times a week etc. It feels like if you don't do all of this so-called self-care must-do, you aren't taking care of yourself correctly.

It's overwhelming.

We get told to do something new or to care about something new all the time. We're just like my prehistorical 2013 Macbook Air, we overheat when we have too many tabs open. It's ok to only pick a couple things to do, to choose only certain things to care about, if it helps you double down on the issue that matters to you. It doesn't make you any less good of a human.

TOXIC TRAITS: COMPARING MY BEHIND THE-SCENES WITH OTHERS' HIGHLIGHT REELS

Social media has made the world a very complicated place to grow up in. Especially when it comes to building self-love. We spend our time comparing ourselves to other people's curated, perfected versions of themselves. We keep putting the bar for greatness higher and higher whether it's what we're supposed to look like when we #wokeuplikethis or how we're supposed to live our lives. And we keep comparing ourselves to these standards, which not even Taylor Swift—who was named artist of the decade in 2019—can measure up to. I don't know Taylor Swift personally (I can still wish) but I'm sure even she opens up her Instagram and feels like she doesn't measure up.

My news feed is full of photos edited with Photoshop, Facetune, or some other random filter app. All these photos that look candid actually come from a full photoshoot where all the elements have been carefully thought out. Everything from the lighting to the decor to the outfit has been planned. Yes, that photo of a person in the snow during the cold winter season, without a jacket, is the result of a long photoshoot. I'll never understand why people would risk pneumonia for a great photo. Maybe it's me who isn't wild enough!

Recently, I asked a friend of mine who always uploads amazing photos to the "gram" what her trick is for getting great shots. She just replied that the trick is to take as many photos as possible. You increase your chances of getting a good one. Then you play with the lighting and the colours. So much for the candid photo snapped spontaneously for the memory, eh?

Most of the things we see online are fake. On some level we all know it's fake.

We've all spent at least five minutes choosing and editing a photo to put online and we aren't even an influencer. Facetune has been downloaded more than 60 million times since its launch. That's insane. Imagine how many edited selfies are out there!

Unfortunately, many of us absorb the content we see on social media as representative of reality without thinking about all the work that has been put behind each photo.

It's ok to do all the work to get a great photo. We all love having those beautiful pictures and memories. What is not ok is thinking that everyone has a better life or is prettier than you while forgetting the truth behind every picture you see. I'm telling you; the girl next door isn't prettier than you when she accidently flips to her front camera on her phone.

When I feel envious of others on social media, I repeat this story to myself.

One day I was at a cafe with a friend and her cousin's friend showed up (what can I say the whole province of Quebec is a small village). She ordered, sat down, took a shot of her newly bought delights, published it, and then left, leaving behind the food and coffee she had just ordered.

I was in shock! I'm not going to explain to you why the coffee and food addict in me considers this action a heinous crime. What I want you to remember from that story is that it is proof that a lot of the content that we consume on social media is often distorted to make us believe in a "perfect life."

During the last few years, I was aware I had every opportunity to be happy but, despite this, I was not.

One of the main reasons was that I spent a lot of energy comparing myself to others on social media. I was comparing my whole life to a few pictures carefully chosen by other people. I compared myself to people who weren't in the same chapter as me in their book. They were further in their careers, had more life experiences, or were older. They were Olympic athletes, models, public figures, travellers, or entrepreneurs.

Obviously, I, who had just graduated, who had not accomplished anything yet, and who did not have a loonie to my name, felt like something was deeply wrong with me every time I opened my accounts. Slowly, this feeling started to chase me throughout the day. Because of my constant exposure to online content, I came to believe, because of the perfectly retouched photos that circulate, that the lives of others were perfect.

This thinking took over my daily life. It felt like I was the only one who wasn't living like a Kardashian even though it's well-known how staged their public lives are. Well, Mark Zuckerberg and Kevin Systrom might be very, very, very smart but not enough to fool me. *Il y a anguille sous roche! (There's an eel under the rock!).* Nobody is happy all the time or having fun all the time.

The funny thing is that I didn't share any values or ambitions with these people. I didn't admire their specific talents or their accomplishments. That said, this didn't prevent me from putting them on a pedestal and diminishing myself. Social media transformed me into a jealous loser. I want what they have or to do what they do. A person online was going on a trip to Thailand and I asked myself why not me? Why am I not able to go? I had no interest in Thailand. I wouldn't go even if I had the resources. Still, I felt less than good.

A girl posted a photo of her new Gucci handbag. I didn't want a Gucci handbag. What would I do with it? If I had one, I'd probably sell it to pay my student loan or, I don't know, I'd feed an entire family in need for a whole year!

Perhaps, human beings are envious by nature. Perhaps we like to attract pity. Certainly, it is essential to admire. Admiration is what allows us to create dreams and define our goals.

I admire people who get involved in helping others or a global cause. It motivates me to volunteer, to do more. I admire the beauty of art, so I am motivated to learn piano, painting, graphic design, photography; I'm motivated to become more creative. I admire the leadership of CEOs; therefore, I want to build my own business and develop leadership skills. The world is full of people and things to admire and that's what inspires us to push ourselves and do better, to believe we can do better.

It reminds us that we can do the same thing, that we can do just about anything. Those people, the ones you aspire to be like, that's who you should get positively influenced by.

The problem is that social media is transporting us into a passive state where our brain often goes into a weird *vegetative mode*. Exactly like when you're binge watching the fifth episode in a row on Netflix and "Are you still watching?" pops up on the screen. We passively observe what we do not have, belittling ourselves instead of wondering what actions we could take to go after the things that we are genuinely interested in. It is often easier to feel sorry for yourself than to take action to change what is bothering you. However, it is important to remember that the first step toward improving your situation is simply taking action. To feel better you need to stop passively lurking and envying other people's lives and start actively engaging with yours.

Another classic social media problem is that beauty and lust are often idealized, which leads us to admire vanity. Actions taken in connection with vanity push us into an eternal vicious cycle which makes us infinitely empty. There'll always be a more beautiful and richer person than me. This statement is probably just as true for you. Sorry!

I can't be the best in every sphere of my life, but I have come to realize that it's ok. It gives me room to grow. It gives me things to aspire to. And it lets me bond with people who can push me out of my comfort zone to be better.

The advent of social media didn't create comparison. When I was a preteen, I didn't have any social media accounts and I'd still compare myself to Amanda Bynes on the cover of Seventeen or Cosmo Girl magazines. I even bought a few of these magazines to learn her beauty secrets. The "secret" was to butter up her eyelids with some sort of powder blue eyeshadow and a white eyeliner–now, I know the whole 90's style is back but can we never do this again please? Luckily for me I only took her beauty advice and not her life advice. I'm glad she's doing better now.

Comparison is not unique to the *always-on-their-phone* millennial generation.

When I was studying consumer science in university, we learned about Leon Festinger and his theory of social comparison. The theory explains that people tend to evaluate themselves by comparing their ideas and abilities with those of others. We define ourselves through other people and by seeking social approval. And this theory was developed in

1954! That was like way before North America even had colour TV. So, super duper old.

This comparison process begins very early. As far back as I can remember, I have always compared myself to my peers.

At 6 years old, I had this one friend, who, without a doubt, was better than me at drawing. I would look at her drawings and think, “Oh, she’s so much better than me!” I’m ready to bet that her mother was never shy about posting her drawings on the fridge. In my house, it was a struggle to get my work up on the fridge. I liked to draw, but I realized very early on that I had no talent. Or perhaps, as I like to believe, I was making abstract art cool before its time. So *avant-gardiste* of me.

Fortunately, when the day of the elementary school Olympics arrived, I compared my results to others’ and I realized that I was at the front of the pack. In the high jump event, I performed as well as Michael Phelps at the Beijing Olympics (at least that’s how it felt). The only sad thing in this story is that this is a useless skill when it comes to finding a career or a job. I can't imagine being asked what my greatest skill is during an interview and answering firmly and proudly, “I jump super high, I bet I can reach your expectations!” At least I know that if I ever want to make some sort of money out of it, I could always be a part of the next *Cirque du Soleil* event.

So, you’ve no doubt seen a lot of quotes on Instagram telling you that “happiness is found when you stop comparing yourself to others.” You might even have a quote like this framed in your living room or on your desk. The thing is, I don’t think you or I ever stop comparing ourselves.

The trick is to use comparison as a source of positive motivation instead of using it negatively to diminish yourself.

So instead of looking at your friend who just got named one of *Forbes’ 30 under 30*, telling yourself again that life is unfair, ask yourself, "What the hell, why shouldn't this be me?" Start believing that you can do it. Be inspired by others' success instead of jealous. Do you see where I'm going with this?

The process of social comparison helps us to identify what we are good at in society's eyes and thereby validate what we are good at through our own eyes. Yup, sometimes we're all as blind regarding our own values as I was in elementary before getting glasses.

The problem is that the advent of social media has widened the scope of comparison.

Back in the day, a person's social circle was usually made up of fifty to one hundred people. I know, fifty to one hundred people seem like so few by today's standards. Today, our circle of comparison is endless with our hundreds or thousands of friends on Facebook and Instagram, not to mention the horrible discovery feature. Today, we compare ourselves to the whole world and we seek approval from the whole *damn* world. How can I expect to get approval from the whole world when I can't even get the approval of my friends on the guys I date?

Facebook and Instagram have billions of users. Billions of people to compare yourself to.

It's easy to find someone who does so much better than you in what you thought made you unique and impressive by scrolling through your news feed for just five minutes.

Nowadays, our social comparison mechanism seems to devalue by default.

A few years ago, I bought my first car: a cherry red Toyota Yaris. I loved it. If I compared myself to my friends, I had a pretty nifty vehicle. I worked for it, I paid for it, I was proud of it. That is, until I opened my social networks to see hundreds of people my age, or a little younger, who owned an Audi.

You know the classic photo of Starbucks coffee held in a freshly manicured hand with the steering wheel ever so casually fit into the photo so you can see the car model. I would just like to say, "What a stupid photo concept!" Anyway...

Suddenly, my little cherry red car that I was so proud of didn't make me feel so good anymore. I know, terrible. Even more so when you think about the fact that the vehicles those insta-models pose with are probably owned by the girls' parents. But I don't usually analyze photos that deeply when I'm scrolling through my feed. So, I felt bad.

Obviously, people very rarely post a photo of their vehicle when it is ugly. If I had opened my social media that day and seen a ten-year-old Chevrolet, I would probably have continued to appreciate my casserole car more. No, I don't feel better than those who own Chevrolet cars, it's just...have you ever heard a non-American saying they love American cars? I don't think so, they suck.

However, because we only publish the most fabulous things, all I had to compare my car to was luxury cars. So, I decreased my self-worth by comparing myself to those who had better cars than me.

Now, I know this is a little dramatic for an example with a car (it was a very lame example). But don't you worry, I don't put all my self-worth into just one specific thing, neither should you. If you value yourself based on only one thing, when you lose it, you lose everything you think that makes you great.

This example might be material, but I don't think our generation actively compares ourselves just through a material perspective. We tend to compare our life and our lifestyle. We compare the university we went to, the program we studied, the company we work for, the internship we have, the level of fitness we have, how well travelled we are, our accomplishments, or our talent in areas such as sports, hobbies, and activities. Every aspect of ourselves, we compare against others.

It's no wonder that, at 25, I have the confidence of a chihuahua facing down a pit bull.

The saddest thing about self-comparison is that it's hard to stop. It leaves us with one of two equally bad feelings: superiority or inferiority. Yup, you either think you're better than everyone else or that everyone is better than you–neither makes you feel like a good human being. The only way I found to cure this is being self-aware when I compare myself to others and bringing my energy and focus back to becoming a better version of myself. There's nothing more valuable than creating your own measuring stick for tracking your own success.

What's funny is, while we spend our time lurking online and envying other people, wishing we had their smile, their hair, their eyes, their humour, their energy, their intentions, their *smartness*, there are people envying us! Someone out there might even be wishing they had my big calves (but probably not)!

I believe it is important not to use social media without being aware that having constant exposure to this type of content can have an impact on our perception of ourselves and others. It is important to be inspired but not to be fooled by what you see as a representation of true happiness. Remember that the grass is not greener in your neighbour's yard. Grass is only more beautiful where you water it.

When you dream of having someone else's life, that person also dreams of having someone else's life. The only life that will make you happy is the life that you define according to your desires, your values, and your dreams. Drawing a line in your head to separate real life and those carefully curated images online is essential to not losing your identity and forgetting who you are.

Online content makes us feel pressured to succeed, to have a perfect life, to be different (in a good or bad way). I know it, I live with this pressure daily. The only thing that really matters is finding what makes sense to you. You see travel pictures, you want to be on vacation. You see an image of a girl in a bikini, you would like to have her body. You see a couple doing wine tasting in Napa, you wish you had a boyfriend that loves wine tasting. Have you ever stopped to wonder what you wanted without someone showing it to you?

"MY LIFE ISN'T PERFECT, BUT AT LEAST MY FEED IS" - EVERYONE ON SOCIAL MEDIA

I think the problem with social media is that it made *perfection* a norm.

The photos that each of us publishes are a collage of our moments of happiness. So they make our lives appear to others as incredible as they can be. This *perfection* sometimes leads us to forget that these pictures are not necessarily representative of a person's complete story. Meaning that the person who you just saw posting a picture on Instagram at a fancy party in New York City, looking like she's having the time of her life, could have spent the rest of the night in the toilet after getting food poisoning. Look, I don't wish it, but it could happen.

Everyone goes through difficult times. We don't rush to share these types of moments. I like to see our online presence as creating our own avatar. We all develop a persona that gives us the opportunity to show the outside world only what we want to show it. We let others see us only in the way we want to be seen.

For example, I don't want to be seen by others as a *party girl*. If you go to my social networks, the chances that you will find a photo of me with a beer in hand or in a club are quite slim. Unless there's still some 2010 photos of me lost on the dark web. If so, please let me know. It can be our little secret, the one we're hiding from my future husband.

That doesn't mean that I don't drink alcohol, go out to bars, or party with my friends. I do. I'm not "college Annie" anymore, but I go out...sometimes...if it's not too far from home...and it's before 8 pm…and a special occasion...

Someone who does not know me, and who just creeps me online, would likely assume I don't party (and that I'm probably pretty boring). That is exactly what I want people to think. The same goes for the people who you follow that seem to always have it together. You only see what they want you to see. We're all online trying to look like our most awesome and impressive selves. It's almost like our chance to create an ideal version of ourselves. We aren't who we seem to be online, at least not entirely...

Last month, I spent a whole day mourning and crying, telling myself that I was a complete failure and wasted my potential because I didn't know what to do with my life. I felt useless. I had been watching Netflix all day and ordering takeout. Unsurprisingly, I didn't post anything that day because I don't want others to look at me the way I was looking at myself.

We're all lying to each other; we're all playing a game where we are trying to look more impressive online than we're in real life.

Recently, I made an interesting observation. I've noticed that I only publish when I'm happy or when I'm having a good moment. Actually, I publish right after it, because at the moment, I'm too busy living my life (lol, really wish that was always the case).

In contrast, I consume content online during my idle time, during the most mundane moments of my daily life. This is what fueled my pain for a long time without me even realizing it. Let me explain.

I'm on my couch, no makeup, wearing comfy clothes (an old t-shirt I've stolen from an ex), I open my Instagram and then I see models wearing bikinis. Obviously, I feel ugly. I remember that my highlights have grown out for months, that my teeth are crooked, and that my dark circles look exactly like those of a medical student during an exam rush at the end of the semester. Later, it's Friday night and I have nothing to do so I bundle up in my pajamas (which are just a bunch of old t-shirts and sweatshirts from guys I used to date since I don't see the point of buying clothes only I will see). I open my Facebook and I see the stories and posts of my friends who are all having fun. I feel bad, and I feel like I'm not enjoying life enough.

I am at work, doing a job where I don't feel valued, but remain there while finding what I want to do—so I open LinkedIn to pass time. I see that several of my university friends have received promotions in new jobs that definitely seem more interesting than mine. As a result, I get the impression that I am far behind and that I will never have a great career.

In short, what I'm trying to make you understand is that before devouring content that praises a perfect life, a life often far from yours, we are often already in a psychological state which is not ideal for making our social comparisons.

When you're already sad, you'll just go on there, trying to find justification for why you feel bad, and let me tell you, you'll find one.

Scrolling through social media during a quarter-life crisis is the equivalent of shopping for depression, or just a really effective way to make all our problems seem way worse. We grew up overexposed to perfect lives due to our consumption of content on social media, which made us develop the habit of comparing ourselves to others and inevitably devaluing ourselves. It made us believe that if our life is not exactly like the one we see online, something must certainly be wrong with us. We feel insecure. We get insecurities about our life choices and who we are and it makes it so much more difficult to move past them. When you're in a period of unhappiness and insecurity, when you struggle to establish a happy life for yourself, scrolling more, easily makes us feel envy toward what we don't have or are. Obviously, we then feel even worse about ourselves.

We carefully observe our network of friends living their most perfect lives. It seems like all of our peers have three jobs, are involved in two committees, never miss their yoga classes, only cook super healthy food (whatever *healthy* is trendy), have a stable romantic relationship, and travel the world every year. The internet is telling us all that we need to have a great job, stay fit, eat well, be funny, be intellectually curious, and have a hundred interests and passions. If we don't, we're doomed to be less than.

I know if I didn't have a serious talk with myself after being online, I could spend hours feeling sorry for myself and only making this crisis seem endless. Not having what everyone has online does not make you less worthy or less than a person.

It's toxic to go online when you don't know the direction in which you're heading. You look at what everyone's doing and you feel discouraged by everything you come across. When you don't even know where you're heading, the gap between you and others can seem much larger than it really is. You can be anything, (even a princess if you're patient enough to wait until Prince Harry and Meghan Markle's son, Archie, grows up (you do you)), but you can't have everything.

Even if we can rationalize the narrative of content we see on social media as not being 100% true, we can't control our emotional reaction to it. So I guess that's why, for me, after spending time online I just want to give up, go watch Netflix, and take a nap. I get so discouraged by seeing so many people "ahead" of me.

It's important to take time off and be happy in real life, not just online. Do not publish every day and keep some part of your privacy. Make it a habit to look around and appreciate what you have. Appreciate and enjoy your friends, family, and experiences. I always take the time to look at the path I have walked mentally and physically, the jobs I have had, the places I have visited, and the people I have met along the way.

I am extremely lucky and that I wouldn't change my family life for that of anyone.

When I feel badly because I see others succeeding in areas where I do not yet shine, I remind myself that I'm travelling and working remotely and that many people spend their lives trying to do what I'm doing. And that even though it isn't the end place in which I want to be, it's a pretty good place to be in. It quickly brings me back to my state of gratitude.

I decided to no longer use my energy to be like others or envy them for what they have. Instead, I put in the effort to create an incredible life and relationships, and use them as inspiration for what I can do and want to accomplish.

THE POWER OF CONNECTION

So, after spending so many words trying to expose how bad social media is, why am I still using it?

I have no magic answer. It would be easier for me to explain to my mom how to use her iPad for the hundredth time, or why I'm paying for already ripped jeans! The only, and very basic, answer I have to offer you is that social media allows me to be inspired and stay connected with my loved ones, and also to the people who I look up the most to. Despite the many negative aspects, there is a way in which social media can be used positively.

Those platforms are an incredible place to get inspired.

Most of my inspiration for the past few years has come from Pinterest. From new cooking recipes to homemade skincare recipes to decorating ideas, I have access to new inspirations every day and I never get bored. I impress myself and impress my friends every day by using Pinterest, which is probably the only reason why I can *almost* cook.

Facebook and Instagram allow me to share my photos while staying connected with my friends and family. It lets me feel like we still share a life together despite the distance. It also makes it easy to discover and create events.

This space is also incredible since it allows me to follow people around me that I admire, that inspire me to become the person I want to be. I subscribe to people on Instagram who have values in alignment with mine. Every day, they inspire me to meditate, work out, eat well, read, experience news things, and develop more sustainable lifestyle habits. They inspire me to go kick ass. By seeing what they do I learn how to easily integrate various techniques in order to achieve my goals. Being able to watch other people's journeys and how they achieve their goals allows me to convince myself that I too can do it. I can also connect with them and ask for advice. I can digitally make friends with them.

Another important, positive aspect of social media is that it has empowered my generation.

A good number of young dreamers have managed to start a company or a community thanks to these platforms. Whenever I meet someone who has built an online business I am extremely admiring of them. I am in awe of all these entrepreneurs who weren't afraid to get started and let the world know what they are doing and who they are. Before social media, to get a business off the ground you usually had to come from a wealthy family. This is no longer the case and it is incredible. People can design their own job and their own path now.

No matter where you come from or where you studied, almost anything is possible and accessible.

The world is open and connected.

I often hear people tell me they don't like social media because they feel like people are turning themselves into a brand. Branding? I think it's great. It makes it possible to shout your values loud and clear, to be heard, and to meet like-minded people.

Do you need an inspiring example? Look to Sweden's Greta Thunberg, a 16-year-old girl who advocates for climate change. It was the end of August, 2018, the start of the new school year, and Greta decided that she would not go to school until the national election, which was to be held on September 9, 2018. At this moment, Sweden has just experienced the most significant heatwave and forest fires in its history. She sat in front of the parliament building every day during school hours and held a "student strike for climate" sign in her hand. Her goal was to force the government to act on climate change, more specifically, she wanted provisions for the reduction of greenhouse gases in accordance with the Paris Climate Agreement put in place. After the election, she continued to strike every Friday. Greta's story was picked up on social media and went viral, especially on Twitter. On Friday, March 15, 2019, she invited students from around the world to go on a global strike against climate change. All over the world, several institutions suspend classes to allow students to join the movement. Recently, she was nominated for the Nobel Peace Prize to be awarded on October 11, 2019. This story would never have been spread around the world or had such an enormous impact without social media.

The power of social media is unmatched and can have a positive impact if supported by good values. Give yourself permission to use it to your advantage.

YouTube? You can learn anything you want on YouTube. The platform allows you to be informed and to gain knowledge in an interactive and entertaining way, so you retain more. It's an unlimited source of knowledge. Whatever you want to learn, someone, sometimes a professional, has made a video about it on YouTube.

A platform such as LinkedIn also allows you to make a great connection through networking. It gives a unique opportunity to find a mentor for career or life advice or get connected with the person who has the role you dream of having and learn how they ended up there. Dreaming of working for a specific business? Go find that CEO on LinkedIn, slide into his or her DMs. Get to know them and ask them personally to work for them.

Social media should be used positively to empower you. Look online, be inspired, and go for your dream.

Want to share your idea, your passion? Be an influencer. Create your own ecom. Take advantage of social media. There's so much greatness that can come from these platforms. Family and friends get reunited. People find neighbours with the same interest. Communities fundraise money for these in need.

There's really so much greatness with technology in general too. How great is it that we have apps like Google Maps? We don't have to ask some random guys on the street that might take it as an opportunity to ask for your number.

All I'm saying is there might be hope for us to use it for good.

I've never been very present on social media. If you are going to visit my Instagram or Facebook profile, you will quickly realize that it is as festive as the Grinch's lair. Just because I don't publish doesn't mean I don't consume. In truth, I love photos! In my opinion, these are unforgettable memories that we collect and this is the best way to relive those moments. Also, I am slightly vain and I like having beautiful photos. I never like to take pictures simply because I believe I'm extremely unphotogenic. Let me *slightly* rephrase: I look super duper ugly in every photo that was ever taken of me. This is not something new as my entourage kindly tells me, reminding me that the camera cannot capture my charisma.

For years, I refused to appear in front of a camera because I couldn't accept looking bad in a photo, nothing but perfection was good enough. I knew that any photos of me would probably land on social media. I was worried about my image at such a heavy weight. I often got mad at my friends because they posted a hideous picture of me. You know that friend who posts the ugliest picture of you, just because she looks like a 10/10 in the photo. Don't be that friend.

But, at 25, I decided to use social media in a way to assert myself more and increase my self-confidence.

I know, it sounds a little funny. Don't read this the wrong way, I'm not trying to become insta-famous here.

The truth is, I have hundreds of photos on my cell phone that portray incredible moments with incredible friends, but that I never publish. I wasn't sure if they were pretty enough, if they would harmonize well with the aesthetic of my feed, or if they'd receive enough "likes." So, I didn't publish them. I would even ask my friends before publishing if they thought a photo was good enough.

I used to be so stressed because of all of these rules we impose on each other on social media: when to publish, how often, which filter to use.

The most ridiculous thing is that I have deleted photos from social media because they did not receive enough "likes." How sad it is that I let others define the value of my photos, and by the same token, my own value according to "likes."

Can you honestly say you've never done or felt the same?

A few years ago, I was so excited when my photos got 11 likes because the names were turning into numbers. "There," I said to myself, "I have a good photo."

Now, even when I get hundreds of likes on a single photo, it's the same thing. No matter the number it leaves me indifferent. "Likes" on social media are not representative of love or true appreciation. You should only take into consideration what you think and what your loved ones think. If your photo receives a lot of "likes" all the better, it has reached several people. If not, so be it! It's a virtually meaningless number, and it stops there. We definitely need to stop digging for hidden meaning when there's none.

I was not sure if I should share this insecurity. I was a little afraid that you, a person I don't know yet, will find me weird for thinking so much. For having a mini anxiety attack before each publication. Then I realized that I was not alone. I have a bunch of friends who, before sharing a photo on social media, send it to me and wonder if I find it beautiful enough to be published. Sometimes they send me several and ask me to choose the one I prefer.

The reality is that most of us are insecure and share this desire to please others. To a certain extent, the eyes of others weigh heavily on us all when it comes to appearing before the whole world.

Why is that so?

Most people judge. This is why some of us, including me, have fear and insecurities. Like I told you before in the chapter about friendship, if you feel like your friends are not supportive of you, reconsider your *so-called* friends. They should be supportive and proud of you no matter what you do offline and online.

You're always going to have supporters and haters. Just be sure your close friends don't fall in the second category.

Don't be shy to be who you are offline and online.

You should only use social media as a source of inspiration and motivation based on your goals: to try a new activity, a new hobby, a new mission. The choice is yours. It's important to do what you do for yourself and not to look like someone else.

Personally, what has helped me a lot is staying subscribed only to the accounts that inspire me. If an account makes me feel bad about who I am, what I do, what I have or don't have, if I can't help but compare myself, I unsubscribe. It's my way to keep my social space a healthy place for my mental health. You should unfollow accounts that don't benefit you in any way or make you feel bad.

The only comparison you should make is between who you were last year and who you are now (cheesy, I know). I work hard every day, push myself, and try not to measure my success by obsessing over what others are doing.

At 25, I realize that I cannot do everything and, unfortunately, I cannot win everything. Time is limited. I can only try to live my best life. I would never go so far as to mourn the success of others. They have worked hard, and they deserve what they get. I also deserve incredible things, but first I have to work to get them. And if I want to work to get them, I need to get off social media and spend time working toward my goals.

Finding a balance when it comes to using social media is extremely difficult. Whether that means consuming content or sharing it. Our pace of life is dependent on these platforms. We have to stay connected–it's a question of life or death! Do not let social media make your life a constant spiral of depression and your quarter-life-crisis endless, it is important that you stay more connected with your reality.

Here's a list of things to help you get into a healthy relationship with social media (yup, that's possible):

- Don't go online if you feel sad, if you're having a bad day, or if you're not feeling good about yourself. It'll only make it worse. Wait until you feel good again.
- Remind yourself that social media is a collage of people's best moments, accomplishments, and happiness; It's not the whole story. Not everyone has things handed to them on a silver platter.
- Follow only the people that inspire you, not the people who make you feel bad about who you are. Every time I see something online that makes me feel like I'm a boring apple instead of a fabulous strawberry on top of a delicious shortcake, I unfollow them.
- Get connected with people you admire online. Be inspired and inspire. Ask them questions about their life, how they got there, get the positive out of their experiences.
- Beat the fear. Post what you want, stop worrying about what everyone is going to think. That photo is good enough. You have to be you to be real. Don't let yourself be pressured into being loved by the whole world. Don't let everyone make you feel like your life or your pretty face is worth less than anyone else's.
- Limit the time you can access certain social media apps. It's an addiction, you need to know when to stop using it. I personally can't access many apps from 9-5pm and after 9pm. I used to leave my phone at home when I went to study at a coffee shop or at school.

With time, I got better at not checking it all the time and, more importantly, needing it all the time.

- Do some social media detoxing every now and then when you feel overwhelmed. Disconnect from the internet and connect with your reality. Call a friend or a family member, meet someone in real life and ask them how they really feel and let them know how you are despite what you make everyone think online.
- If someone is living a life you aspire to live, DM them! Ask them how they made things happen for themselves. You might realize that they too had to struggle. They might have advice too to help you turn your life around. TRULY connect with those who share your values and visions, seek their advice.
- Remove the apps from your phone and take time off social media to improve yourself by learning new skills and getting into new hobbies. Allow yourself to grow and let go of trying to impress your followers. You might be really good at something you haven't even tried yet, but you wouldn't know because you're too busy lurking online. These new things are what will make you happy.

Use social media in a way that makes you the happiest about being yourself and having the life you have. Remember that no matter how in debt you get into by going on expensive vacations or restaurants to impress strangers on Instagram, it'll never make you love your own life. No matter how many filters you put on your face and how much you Photoshop your body, it'll never make you love yourself. Unplug yourself so you can better connect with what truly matters: the people around you and your inner self.

So please, make a pact with me, you cool human! You're obviously cool because you're reading my book!

Let's pinky swear to be more authentic online so we can look out for the wellbeing of one another. Every time we're being inauthentic online, we're acting out of vanity, for the likes, the followers and the status. And every time, we're negatively impacting the view someone has of themself. We're pressuring each other into perfectly curated lives that don't exist. Mental health is health. And it's about time we do something about it.

A pact for a happier life!

It's unfair that I feel shitty when I go online. I know you might think unfair is a strong word and that I'm just showing an attitude because of my French heritage (you're not wrong), but it isn't fair at all. I'm not the only one who's struggling at work, who's love life could use a little bit more of "ouh là là!" and who's alone on Saturday night.

Nobody should feel this way, ever!

Let's stop making each other feel bad, or less than. Let's stop lying online. Let's stop exaggerating our life in our pictures and status updates like we exaggerated on our resume. Let's stop hiding the averageness of our life. Let's stop playing this wicked little game that we've been playing since we had our first MSN messenger account.

Yes, this little game started a long time ago, when we set our MSN status as "ShOpPiNg In QuEbEc CiTy WiTh My BeStiEe!!" or when we used to set our Facebook relationship status to "It's complicated" all to make our life seem cooler. Or was that just me?

Let's stop making each other worried about the aesthetic of our feed, the frequency of our posts, the number of likes or followers we have, the quality of our iPhone camera, or the exoticness of our travel. Let's stop making each other ask if it's "gram worthy" or a "good time to post". Let's stop making each other wonder if we're worthy at all.

Let's be honest with ourselves and each other. We are the one making all of these stupid rules anyway.

Let's be honest so we can all stop pressuring ourselves and each other to reach unrealistic standards. And then, maybe, we can start being happy online again. Maybe, we can start being kind to ourselves again.

I promise to keep bragging and posting selfies and photos of friends, family, dogs, food, activities, and travel. I promise to not lie, exaggerate, or embellish the truth. I promise to be real online:

Name: Annie-Claude Ouellet

Date: 2019-11-21

Name: ______________________

Date: ______________________

NOW WHAT? THIS IS THE CONCLUSION

Wow. I've just written a book. And someone (you) has made it all the way to the end. Congrats!

Honestly, I had doubts anyone would make it through. It's a pretty amazing feeling both for you and for me. For me because it feels like I've finally achieved something that can justify the insane amount of "perseverance trophies" I've been ashamed of collecting over the years. And for you because you can finally cross reading this from your to-do-list. Please, tell me I'm not the only one who thinks that crushing things from a to-do-list is as satisfying as popping your partner's pimples (not your own obviously, who want to self inflict that pain).

If everything went as I expected, you probably had fun reading this, but now it's coming to an end, so you rightfully want to know: how do you actually get over your quarter-life crisis?

Lucky for you, I'm about to spill my tea.

When my quarter-life crisis hit me I was miserable. Every job out there seemed far from exciting. Things that I used to enjoy, like working out, felt more than mundane, and hanging out with friends was a chore. I felt like I was carrying an empty heart and soul all day long. I wasn't depressed per se, but I felt lonely all the time.

I thought if I could find my passion or my purpose, it would miraculously liberate me from my miserable life. With a passion or a purpose, I could get a job I was passionate about, one that I could thrive at. Since I would be thriving at it, I'd finally get a decent salary, so I would have time and money to spend on hobbies and travelling. I'd be happy, stress free, and I could finally enjoy time with my friends. That was a very naïve and hedonistic thought. There's no such thing as a quick fix to your life. In fact, there's this notion in psychology called the hedonic treadmill, which is the tendency of humans to maintain a relatively stable level of happiness in spite of major positive or negative events or life changes. Which means, there's no quick fix to a higher level of happiness.

So, when are we happy? I mean really happy, like your mom when she invites you for dinner after cooking your favourite meal.

According to Gandhi, "Happiness is when what you think, what you say, and what you do are in harmony." The smaller the gap between what you should do, or say you need to do, and what you actually do, the happier you will be. This means that in order for us to be happy, we need to start chasing the life we want, we need to close the gap.

I believe happiness—true, long-lasting happiness—is determined by two things: your mindset i.e., your attitude and outlook on life; and your actions and goals.

After reading a crazy number of self-help books, and doing a whole lot of soul searching to diagnose the cause of my quarter-life crisis, the prescription to get over it seems pretty simple: goal setting and taking action. I wouldn't necessarily call myself a genius, but it did work.

When you have a quarter-life crisis, or any existential crisis really, something has to trigger it. Maybe it's a job (the one that makes you dream about Friday coming, the one you only keep because you need to pay your bills) or a relationship (the person you're dating only because they always have free Chipotle coupons) that makes you feel prisoner in your own life. Sometimes you follow a path because it made sense at the beginning, but then it starts to feel like you're on auto-pilot and things are just happening to you, which makes you feel a little claustrophobic. But the good news is you're in the driver's seat. You choose what direction you want to travel in and, if you feel like you've taken a wrong turn, you can always just turn around! Or maybe it's a lack of vision for your life. When you're in university, your vision is pretty clear: get through the semester, get through the year, finish your degree. After graduation, we start living in a text-to-text, story-to-story, post-to-post, bills-to-bills world. We rush and get sucked up into the now, and don't often take time to take a step back and look at the vision we have for our life.

A quarter-life crisis is a chance to rebuild, or build, a life that coincides with your interests, passions, and values. It's a good kick in the butt, and you should make the most out of this opportunity to turn your life around.

To do so, the first step is being self-aware. If you feel like something is going incredibly wrong with your life, like you could've written one of Adele's songs, sit down and list all the things that you're unhappy about. I know you're thinking this is just more BS advice from one of the people you went to high school with who's now in a pyramid scheme, but please bear with me a little longer here.

Once you're done with that (hopefully not too long) list, write down how you want things to be instead. Actually, write down everything you wish to do or accomplish in life. This is not a graded assignment, and I promise nobody will see it, so don't hold back. Think about your small dreams, your big dreams, and all the ones in between. Think about the things you have always wanted to learn or accomplish. Think about the person you are, and the person you want to become. Slowly, these things will morph into a vision of the life you could have.

Then, you can start setting goals to fill the gap between where and who you are now, and where you want to go and who you want to be—remember that you can choose the direction you want your life to go to. Whether you struggle with a sense of direction, or with making big changes in your life, setting goals will help. At this point, set an extraordinary goal, because you can and why the hell not! Making goals for the next 10 years will be hard at first—ok, it'll be close to impossible. But you're not obliged to have that big of a long time vision. But there are no rules here; you can just start small. You can start by setting goals for the next 30 days, the next 6 months, the next year. After that, maybe you can set them for the next 5 years. No need to sweat like you're at a crowded musical festival on a hot day; nothing is set in stone, it's ok to change your goals as you evolve. You must certainly change them, actually. You just need something to start working with to guide your decision and actions. Inaction is the only way you can actually mess up in your twenties.

Yes, I've talked about it a lot in the book, but the secret is just goal setting.

Look, I know setting goals can be overwhelming. Sometimes we avoid setting goals because we're scared of setting ourselves up for failure, and if we all have one thing in common, it's that we all hate failing. But it's also the only way to set yourself on the path toward change and success. Setting goals is important, it gives you a benchmark to hold yourself accountable to, something to drive you forward each day. Goals are also amazing because they give you a vision, and make you focus more on achieving them and less on comparing yourself to others. Remember, the fantastic lives you see portrayed on social media are probably fake...

Only you can achieve the goals you set for yourself. Yup, not even your dad can make them happen for you. Too often, we seek clarity *before* taking any actions, but I think clarity actually comes *from* taking actions. So, if you want to learn how to play piano, buy yourself a keyboard, take a class online, and make a commitment to practice every Sunday morning at nine. The more specific the goal, the easier it'll be to hold yourself accountable to it. When you don't hold yourself accountable, you're letting yourself down. That's the worst thing you can possibly do.

There really isn't much magic to building the life you want. It just takes getting started moving toward a better place. Actions are all that matter, since you're in control of the situation you're in. Have some personal agency, pumpkin; don't let the basic girl inside you keep screaming, "*I can't even!!*"

Change doesn't happen because of one big action, and success doesn't happen overnight. Your uncle Vernon (*Oh man, not him again!*) told you over and over that Rome wasn't built in a day. You can't build a perfect summer body by doing six sit ups a year and reaching for a box of Thin Mints every night (what can I say, I may need an intervention for my addiction to Thin Mints). Success happens through small actions that take place in our everyday lives—the ones we call habits. Habits determine who you are and the kind of life you live one step at a time, over and over again. And that's ok, baby steps are sexy too. There's no elevator to the life you want so, if you want to get there, you have to take the stairs. Writing a book starts with a line. Being fit starts with a single set of push ups. Becoming a painter starts with one stroke on the canvas. Developing your intellectual curiosity starts with reading a book. It starts with one thing that we do over and over again.

One habit that we keep ourselves accountable to, and over time becomes part of who we are. That's how in a year or five from now, you'll wake up a writer, an athlete, a painter, or a well-read individual.

Goals don't have to be overwhelming. Habits are easy to implement if you make them easy. You can combine them with something else you already do. For example, journaling while you're sipping on your overpriced morning coffee. Or setting your environment in a way that makes your routines easy, like putting your clothes and running shoes out before snuggling into bed at night, so it's easier to go for a run in the morning (at least, that makes it easier for me to ensure my morning self lives up to the ambition of my nighttime self). With time, you'll do these things without thinking, they'll become a part of you.

Through this method of goal setting, then turning actions into habits, which causes a mindset shift, I've now written a book (yay!), learned Spanish (¡Hurra!), lived in Australia (cheers, mate!) and I'm now on my way to reading a book a week for a year. And I feel more fulfilled. Still not as much as when my dog comes to hang out with me by himself (I go crazy over a cute cavalier King Charles), but it's a start, eh?

Knowing if you're doing well in life is hard now that we don't get gold star stickers or trophies for participation. Taking actions or keeping up with habits that bring us closer to our goals are the best ways to measure how we're doing. You might not achieve everything you set out to do, you might not have completed the same milestones everyone else your age, but as long as you're taking actions or building habits that bring you closer to what you define as success, as long as you're growing, know you're doing more than just awesome! You're awe-inspiring.

While you're working toward your goals, surround yourself with good friends, with people who lift you up. Give them a call, tell them how you're REALLY feeling (by that I mean quit trying to impress everyone, be raw, be vulnerable, be real). Seek advice from people who live the life you want to live. I truly believe one of the best skills to have is knowing when and how to ask for help. And if it all feels too much, go see a qualified therapist. Not because you're hopeless but because therapy works, duh!

Be aware of how you spend your time. Your environment and your mindset are everything. Friends influence who you are, how you act, how you think, and what you care about and value. Spend lots of time with people who inspire you. Pay attention to what kind of content you consume; social media might impact your mood and how you perceive yourself. Value your time; reading a book will (almost) always be better than binge watching Netflix. You'll feel much better—it's like a facial for the soul.

Let go of the pressure of having it all figured out. Make the best decision using the best resources you can find, you can always readjust later.

Think big for yourself and believe in something bigger than yourself. You can do whatever you set your mind to. Stop looking at things as they are but as they could be. Your perspective also makes you who you are. If you think you're worthy, confident, and capable, you will act in that fashion.

Be kind to yourself about the place you are now. What you're feeling is normal. When you've been raised with no adversity in life, it might take some extra work to navigate the rough patches. It's totally normal that you feel overwhelmed by everything.

And remember, you're not alone in this; there are hundreds, thousands of us struggling in this post-grad blues, trying to grow up and cross the mess out of "hot mess." It's okay to be low key pissed at all those people on Instagram who just bought houses straight out of *The Home*

Improvement Channel, just got married to the French version of Zac Effron, just went on *another* vacation to the Cayman Islands, and just landed the job they were dreaming of straight out of university. Just don't let the (perceived) success of others distract you from achieving your own success.

Your life is yours to design. You're too big for the life you're in right now. It's time to become a doer, and do to your life what Jane Fonda did to the fitness industry.

You've got this pumpkin, I pinky swear!

ON THE BOOKSHELF OF A QUARTER-LIFE CRISIS SURVIVOR

- *The Defining Decade: Why Your Twenties Matter—And How to Make the Most of Them Now* - Meg Jay
- *Time And How We Spend It: The 7 Rules For Richer, Happier Days* - James Wallman
- *Atomic Habits* - James Clear
- *Daring Greatly* - Brené Brown
- *The War of Art* – Steven Pressfied
- *I Will Teach You to Be Rich* – Ramit Sethi

THANKS TO...

Cliff, for helping me believe, everyday, that I can do things that are bigger than myself—you make it easier to face the world. The world needs more *Cliff*. Thanks for reading all of my scrappy unfinished first drafts, and part of my very own journal as I tried to make something out of it.

Meghan, for making this book happen; you magically made all my messy ideas hold together, and made sure they all came across in my own voice. You surely did find the "every word" to my words. Thanks for your honesty, your criticism, and for proofreading (I think the readers should know I still struggle with *than* and *then*).

Karine, for putting into colours and illustrations the essence of this book. If this is the only book I ever write, I'll happily show off the design until the day I die.

Annie-Claude Ouellet is native of Quebec, Canada. Growing up, she lived a very sheltered life, only having to worry about which new dress to wear at her next figure skating competition. After graduating from Laval University, she started actively chasing down more meaning in life — desperately trying to understand her place in the world. With a ton of existential questions to answer, she became an avid reader and a self-development enthusiast, and aspires to become an unstoppable goal-getter. She wears her basicness on her sleeves and she is always on the lookout for new adventures and her next *grande* chai latte.

Made in United States
North Haven, CT
15 January 2022